the BINGE FREEDOM METHOD™

YOUR FOUR-PILLAR PLAN TO BEAT EMOTIONAL EATING FOR GOOD

MARCELLE ROSE

Illustrations by Leslie Mello

Printable workbook and bonus resources can be accessed at:
https://marcellerosenutrition.co.uk/book-resources

the BINGE FREEDOM METHOD™

PARK HALL
PUBLISHING

PRAISE FOR THE BINGE FREEDOM METHOD™

The Binge Freedom Method is a comprehensive framework offering hope, guidance, and science backed practical strategies to overcome binge eating and emotional eating. This insightful book provides a clear path to reclaiming control and finding lasting freedom from food struggles.

NICKI WILLIAMS, AUTHOR OF 'IT'S NOT YOU, IT'S YOUR HORMONES'

This Book is an exceptional and intuitively practical guide for anyone who struggles with emotional eating, or is supporting someone who is. Marcelle expertly reveals her proven approach to beating binge & emotional eating in an insightful and compassionate style, which may support anyone to discover a better relationship with food and an overall improved wellbeing.

JINTY & LOU HOSTS OF THE WOMENKIND COLLECTIVE PODCAST

I highly recommend Marcelle's inspiring and practical guide to support you on your journey in overcoming binge eating. Marcelle offers a comprehensive and expertly guided pathway, built around her four pillars (Nourish, Balance, Think and Feel) to support you on your healing journey. It is brought to life with relatable client case studies and actionable steps along the way. You definitely need this in your toolkit in binge eating recovery.

HARRIET FREW, THERAPIST & HOST OF THE EATING DISORDER THERAPIST PODCAST

Empowering and insightful, this book provides the tools you need to reclaim control over your relationship with food.

KATE HUDSON-HALL THERAPIST AND AUTHOR OF "ANXIETY HACKS"

ABOUT MARCELLE ROSE

Marcelle Rose is an award-winning specialist in emotional and disordered eating, a BANT Registered Nutritionist, and a coach. She helps women overcome binge eating, bulimia, emotional eating, and yo-yo dieting so they can reclaim their lives.

Early in her career, whilst working as a registered nutritionist and health coach, Marcelle was approached by a growing number of clients struggling with emotional eating, binge eating, and yo-yo dieting and wanted to investigate new approaches to help. This prompted her to train as a Master Practitioner of Eating Disorders and Eating Distress with the renowned National Centre for Eating Disorders. She gained expertise in disordered eating, combining eating psychology and behaviour change with her nutritional therapy practice. Marcelle continues to expand her knowledge through regular courses with eminent psychologists, focusing on body image and behaviour change to adapt and incorporate new techniques into her work.

Since specialising in this area, Marcelle has worked with hundreds of clients, achieving remarkable results. Her philosophy is to help people transform their eating behaviours and relationships with food for the long term, without dieting or food restriction. She advocates for balance, enjoying food without shame or guilt, and fostering self-acceptance and empowerment.

Marcelle wrote this book to share her approach and help more people reclaim their lives. She consults with clients nationwide and worldwide and supports women in her free Facebook community, The Food Freedom Collective.

Join her community here:

https://www.facebook.com/groups/
thefoodfreedomcollectivewithmarcellerose

This book is dedicated to the memory of Jess, an extraordinary soul who touched the lives of all who knew her.
Jess, your presence is deeply missed but your memory will be cherished forever and always shines brightly in everything we do.

CONTENTS

introduction

What has Led You Here?

If you have picked up this book, then I'm going to assume you are struggling with your eating. It's likely you experience feelings of shame and guilt around food and have been in an on-and-off relationship with diets throughout your life, every time feeling a failure because you have 'blown it', often culminating in one or more episodes of uncontrolled eating. Perhaps you are constantly thinking about food, your body, or diets, your mind cluttered with the endless inner chatter that takes over everything.

Are You an Emotional Eater?

Most people emotionally eat from time to time, but difficulties arise when this becomes your sole coping mechanism, to numb feelings or where you seek solace from discomfort. Often the initial sense of relief, comfort, or pleasure triggered by the reward centre in your brain swiftly transforms to feelings of guilt and shame. These emotions impact how you feel about yourself, your confidence, and self-worth, keeping you stuck in a never-ending cycle.

Your eating habits might involve continuous grazing, alternating between food restriction and eating large amounts, or you may face challenges around eating during certain times of the day. You might identify yourself as a comfort or stress eater, label yourself a food addict, or believe you are addicted to particular foods.

So, What is Binge Eating?

Binge eating is characterised by eating a large amount of food within a short period of time, often associated with a loss of control[1]. The eating episode does not provide any pleasure for the individual. Many describe it as being in a "trance-like" state. Often a binge is followed by periods of restricted eating to compensate for what has been consumed.

Other Signs and Symptoms:

- Eating faster than you normally would
- Obsessing over food, sometimes planning the binge in advance
- Eating until you are overfull, uncomfortable or even sick
- Eating large amounts of food when you are not physically hungry
- Eating in secret
- Feeling distress, shame, and self-loathing after a binge

Overcoming binge and compulsive eating not only frees you from the daily torment of managing your eating habits but also serves as a profound act of self-care for your body and overall well-being.

The ramifications of binge and compulsive eating extend beyond the emotional and psychological toll, which may result in heightened anxiety, depression, social isolation, an increased risk of substance abuse, and diminished self-worth.

Physically, these eating patterns can manifest in sleep disturbances, weight gain, hypertension, cardiovascular disease, Type 2 diabetes, digestive problems, and musculoskeletal pain. In extreme cases, the risk of intestinal perforation during a binge episode could potentially lead to fatal consequences if intestinal contents leak into surrounding tissues.

Over the past decade, my work has been specifically dedicated to helping hundreds of clients liberate themselves from the 24/7 thoughts about food, their weight or shape, and never feeling good enough. I've observed first-hand the profound impact these eating and thought patterns have on peoples' daily lives, but I also know that it is possible to break free. My mission is to provide support to as many people as I can reach, offering both hope and practical solutions to overcome these challenges. This has compelled me to write this book and share my approach widely.

I want you to know that you are not alone. It's estimated that one in fifty people struggle with binge eating disorder (BED) and that is just those who meet the tightly defined criteria and have an official diagnosis. There are many more people who battle with disordered eating of which bingeing is a factor. It often goes undiagnosed and hidden from others.

You may be thinking that it isn't possible for you to create the change in your life that you want, but I can tell you, hand on heart, that it can be done. You can build a happy relationship with food, make peace with your body, and stop emotional eating and bingeing for good.

Don't get me wrong, it takes work, but not the type that the diet industry would have you do such as following rigid rules, and diet plans, and restricting certain foods. *The Binge*

Freedom Method™ will help you to understand yourself – your behaviour patterns, thoughts, and emotions – and become aware of your eating experience without judgement. You will learn about what needs are not being met and how to nourish your body and mind whilst being able to take joy and pleasure from food.

This book serves as your guide. Using my method, you will feel supported every step of the way, by helping you to build autonomy and trust in yourself and your body. As you progress, you'll acquire the skills, using the tools and strategies provided, to become your *own* coach in order to make lasting change.

The Road Ahead

It's important to note that this journey is never linear. There will be ups and downs, and this is normal and to be expected. Think of it as a long bicycle ride. At times, you may hit a bump or obstacle in the road and fall off your bike.

In these instances, it's critical to hop straight back on again. Recognise that doing this does not mean starting from square one. Instead, it's about dusting yourself off and continuing your journey from where you left off. If you have a setback, it doesn't mean that you have failed and need to start again. This is in fact where the learning begins.

THE HEALING JOURNEY

What people expect

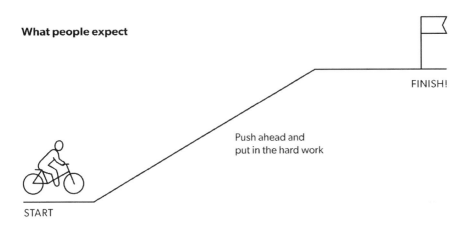

FINISH!

Push ahead and
put in the hard work

START

What it usually feels like

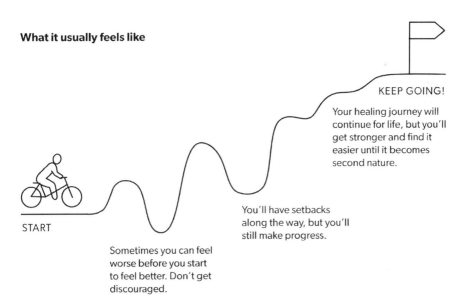

KEEP GOING!

Your healing journey will
continue for life, but you'll
get stronger and find it
easier until it becomes
second nature.

You'll have setbacks
along the way, but you'll
still make progress.

START

Sometimes you can feel
worse before you start
to feel better. Don't get
discouraged.

Why It's Not About the Weight

I understand that dissatisfaction with your body weight or size may be providing the motivation to embark on this journey[2]. This is often why so many people have a long dieting history but are not able to break the pattern of binge or emotional eating[3]. However, it is critical to understand that a weight-focused approach will only keep you stuck in an endless dieting cycle and your eating behaviours will resurface soon enough[4] [5].

Weight gain is a symptom of binge and emotional eating but not the cause of it. Yes, I often see weight loss occur as a side effect of overcoming the eating behaviours, but it is not helpful to target it.

You can spend your entire life trying to shrink your body, or instead you can choose freedom.

The Binge Freedom Method™ will focus on how you feel in your body – appetite, cravings, energy, mood – rather than a number on the scales as you work on your relationship with food.

Is Compulsive Eating a Sign of Food Addiction?

There is an emerging theory that food can be addictive, causing changes in the brain similar to those seen with drug addiction. Researchers have found that food manufacturers design foods to increase consumption, creating hyper-palatable products that can override our natural satiety signals[6]. Feeling addicted to certain foods is a valid experience and can manifest as addiction-like behaviours.

However, many experts question the legitimacy of equating compulsive eating with drug or alcohol addiction[7]. Strong cravings for certain foods are linked to biological drives that vary from person to person, especially if you've been restricting specific foods, labelling them as "good" or "bad", or undereating.

When you attempt to eliminate binge-type foods from your diet, you might find yourself obsessing about them constantly. Once you succumb to the craving and begin eating these foods, you may feel unable to stop and feel utterly out of control. However, experts believe this is not the same as the experiences associated with substance abuse.

One of the problems with the 'food addiction' model is that we cannot abstain from food, as we can from alcohol and drugs. The theory overlooks all factors that contribute to binge and emotional eating. Additionally, studies show that you actually become less interested in a food the more often you are exposed to it, leading to reduced cravings for that food[8], contradicting the idea that binge foods must be eliminated forever.

Therefore, while certain foods can elicit addiction-like responses, adopting a deprivation mindset is counterproductive. Conversely, by addressing the key underlying factors outlined in this book, you will heal your relationship with food, overcome your eating behaviours, and eventually be able to feel comfortable around all foods, without the need for restriction.

Where to Begin
The Binge Freedom Method™ consists of four sections, each representing one of the four pillars required to instigate change. These sections are interconnected, no one pillar is more important than the others. Throughout each section of the book, you will find *actions steps* along with a comprehensive summary of an *action plan*, where you can

keep track of your progress. It is essential to commit to the process by working through each action step and using the tools and resources provided. Simply reading the book, without taking action, will not be enough to bring about transformative change in your life.

THE FOUR PILLARS

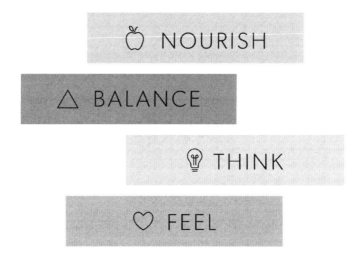

Based on my experience of helping countless clients, I have found that the first pillar, Nourish, is a good place to start. By addressing how to nourish your body first, it is possible to bring about significant reductions in the physiological reasons behind cravings early in the process.

The second pillar will help you balance the key physical systems that influence your appetite and cravings and shape your eating patterns. Within Balance, you'll discover how your brain chemicals, hormones, gut microbiome, circadian rhythm (and more) impact your eating behaviours and how to support them within your body.

When you move on to the third pillar, *Think*, you will address your thinking and beliefs about food, dieting, and your body and tackle ingrained habits. By addressing your mindset, you will learn how to create long-lasting, positive change to your eating behaviour.

The final pillar, *Feel*, is focused on understanding the impact your emotions have on your eating habits and cravings. You'll gain insights into regulating difficult feelings and develop new, more helpful coping mechanisms.

Don't forget to join my free Facebook group *The Food Freedom Collective* for additional support whilst you embark on this journey.

https://www.facebook.com/groups/
thefoodfreedomcollectivewithmarcellerose

Printable versions of all downloadable resources can be found at:

https://marcellerosenutrition.co.uk/book-resources

A Note on Trauma

Individuals who have experienced trauma are far more likely to engage in disordered eating[9]. The earlier the trauma occurs, the more severe its impact tends to be. Disordered eating of any kind is not solely about food but rather serves the individual as a means to gain control over specific areas of their life when they feel overwhelmed or helpless.

You may have employed restrictive or overeating behaviours as a way to manage and conceal feelings of shame, hopelessness, or a lack of control following a traumatic event. These eating behaviours may be providing you with a feeling of security whilst distancing yourself from the pain that others may not even realise has deeply affected you.

It is possible that your eating habits have become so deep rooted that you may have forgotten the reasons behind them in the first place.

If you have experienced trauma and it has not been addressed, I strongly recommend seeking targeted psychological intervention such as CBT or EMDR, as this trauma could potentially hinder your progress.

pillar one: nourish

The first pillar is called *Nourish*. The objective of this part of the book is to guide you to make practical changes to your diet that will support your body's physiological needs. This approach will help you to plan balanced meals, whilst dispelling false notions and misconceptions about food. By embracing these principles, you will feel more satisfied after eating and transition towards stable eating patterns with confidence.

1. DEBUNKING DIET MYTHS

I get it. One of the biggest challenges you face is feeling overwhelmed and confused the more you search for the solution to your eating difficulties. Google 'healthy eating' and it can take you down a very deep, dark rabbit hole of conflicting information. So, where should you even begin when it comes to managing your diet?

Before you start, it's important to understand why you remain trapped in this cycle of eating and self-loathing. Both dieting and preoccupation with weight and shape are important risk factors for the development of binge and emotional eating[10] [11] [12]. In fact, around a third of the people seeking weight loss treatments have symptoms of binge eating disorder.

My clients often share how they began dieting as early as 11 or 12 years old, and this pattern then persisted throughout their lifetime. Emotional eating or bingeing often stems from some form of food restriction[13]. Ultimately, it's the body's method of protecting you against a perceived famine. The body responds by raising your hunger hormones prompting you to search for food and this leads to intense cravings. Given the abundance of fad diets and weight loss rules and trends, it's understandable if you've thought, *this diet will be different*, each time you've embarked on a new one.

We are constantly bombarded with dieting and weight loss myths, based on poor-quality evidence (if any at all). These include misconceptions such as calories in equals calories out and that fats and carbs will make you fat. We will explore this further below. These fallacies have become so ingrained that they are rarely questioned, playing into the diet industry's agenda. This multibillion-pound industry profits from making women believe that their worth is tied to a specific size, weight, or shape. It perpetuates the notion that women must diet in order to conform to a 'thin body ideal'. Diet companies and so-called experts want to sell you their diet and have no qualms about cherry-picking research to convince you of its effectiveness. The problem is that dieting doesn't work and leads to a disconnection from our body and what it really needs.

Now, let's unravel the various types of diets and demystify common myths about them.

Calorie deficit diets

How many times have you heard the saying – you simply need to burn more calories than you consume to lose weight? However, the energy we consume and then burn in calories is only a small part of the picture[14]. When we rely on a simple physics equation, we ignore the fact that each of us is unique. We have complicated regulatory systems that control appetite regulation, fat metabolism, and energy expenditure which, to some extent, are influenced by our genetics. An individual's health history where conditions like hypothyroidism and PCOS (polycystic ovary syndrome), specific medications, and digestive issues, as well as differences in stress levels and sleep patterns, will impact body weight.

Weight management involves a complex interplay between hormones, brain chemistry, gut ecosystem, energy demands, available energy sources, genes, and numerous other variables.

Calorie deficit diets also overlook the fact that food is much more than simply calories[15]. It consists of macronutrients (carbohydrates, protein, and fats), micronutrients (minerals and vitamins), as well as phytonutrients (natural compounds in plants that have beneficial effects on health), and enzymes that aid digestion and nutrient absorption. All of these components interact with our biology in diverse and complex ways.

Counting calories is an unreliable and fruitless exercise. It fosters an unhappy relationship with food, often leading to emotional eating, bingeing, guilt, and self-deprecation[16].

Your body needs *enough* food to sustain efficient functioning of your metabolism. Your subconscious brain will do everything it can to control how much fat your body stores. If you undereat then your basal metabolic rate (BMR) will be switched downwards – slowing down the rate at which it burns energy[17] [18]. This is something you may be able to override for a short period of time (e.g. during the honeymoon period of a diet), but for most people any weight loss will not be long lasting.

Frequently, calorie restrictive diets are disguised as something else, such as those that involve counting points or meal replacement drinks, but any diet involving a reduced calorie intake falls into this category.

Fasting diets
Intermittent-fasting diets include time-restricted eating, where the daily eating window is limited, and periodic fasting, which significantly restricts calorie intake for several days each week.

A recent study[19] examined individuals currently practising fasting, past fasters, and those who had never fasted. The study revealed that past and current fasters were significantly more prone to episodes of binge eating compared to those who had never practised fasting. This aligns with what I see with my clients: binge eating is a consequence of fasting and does not just go away. Additionally, intermittent fasting diets may lead to fatigue, reduced focus, muscle mass loss during physical activity, and intense hunger. There is insufficient evidence to suggest that weight loss outcomes from fasting diets are any better than those of calorie restrictive diets[20].

Low-fat and low-carb diets

Both of these types of diets are problematic. Low-fat diets deny you the satiating fats that help you to feel fuller for longer[21]. Eating naturally occurring fats (as opposed to added fats) enhances satisfaction from your meals, activating satiety receptors in your brain (signals that regulate feelings of fullness and satisfaction), and making your food more enjoyable[22]. Low-fat diets often promote fat-free products that are packed with various additives, including sweeteners to improve the palatability of the food. Furthermore, low-fat diets deny you of the essential omega-3 fats which can accelerate metabolism and help to burn calories[23]. They also provide important health benefits throughout your body, which include supporting heart health, improving cognitive function, and reducing inflammation.

Low-carb diets often involve eliminating whole grains which are an important energy source, rich in fibre and abundant in the essential nutrients that help to curb sugar cravings. Fibre plays a pivotal role in regulating blood glucose levels, promoting satiety and keeping sugar cravings at bay[24].

Though it is helpful to switch refined 'white' carbohydrates for whole grains, low-carb advocates tend to exclude all types of carbohydrates, leading to diets devoid of all grains, and sometimes even fruit and vegetables too.

Bear in mind that for your metabolism to function effectively, your body must not be deprived of any food group. If you find yourself avoiding certain food groups due to their calorie content or from following a restrictive diet, you're likely to be missing out on key nutrients that are critical for your metabolism to function at its best. These practices become unsustainable in the long term and will leave you with a sense of failure when you inevitably 'fall off the wagon'.

You might convince yourself that you are not on a diet if you haven't joined the latest diet trend. However, if you are measuring food, counting calories, fasting, detoxing, or restricting foods or food groups then this is dieting behaviour.

The big diet companies are recognising that there is increased awareness about the ineffectiveness of weight-loss diets. They have found cunning ways to disguise weight-loss programmes, apps, and books as 'healthy eating plans' and many ironically claim that 'this is not a diet' (so do watch out for those).

A Note on Weight Stigma

There is no doubt that weight stigma is widespread in our society, evident within government policy, healthcare settings, the media, workplaces[25] (including wage disparities and promotion biases)[26], and education. There is a common misconception that a person's body weight is determined by their individual choices and that it can be easily addressed by 'eating less and moving more'. This stigma has an emotional, psychological, and physical impact[27] on those with larger bodies, leading to increased stress and calorie intake[28], emotional eating, and binge eating[29].

Diet culture permeates all aspects of our lives, from the content we encounter in newspapers, magazines, and on social media, to the influence of our caregivers and family, leading to the internalisation of negative attitudes towards body size[30].

As we grow up, we often encounter stereotypes where larger people are portrayed as villains in cartoons or employed as comic characters in movies[31]. In healthcare settings weight is frequently prioritised as a primary concern, regardless of the individual's health status.

Whether you are in a larger body or even a smaller one, if you harbour an intense fear of gaining weight, your thoughts may be rooted in anticipation of facing rejection, judgement, or feeling unlovable.

I want you to know that your feelings are valid. However, it is important to offer yourself compassion if you've encountered stigma and don't let external influences steer you off course.

2. THE TRUTH ABOUT YOUR WEIGHT

Is reaching your 'magic' weight extremely important to you? Have you set a weight goal based on what you weighed in the past or what you think you should weigh? The diet industry leads us to believe that we can all achieve any weight goal we set for ourselves. We see before and after photos and think: *if they can do it why can't I? Surely, it's just about willpower?*

The reality is that your body has a powerful regulation system that maintains your weight within a relatively narrow range. This weight range, known as the set point, fluctuates throughout your life, notably as you get older[32]. Research indicates that most people's set point shifts higher each time they go on a diet[33]. This means that after the end of a diet you could weigh more than when you started.

When you yo-yo diet – repeatedly losing weight, regaining it, then losing weight again – your starting weight will step up each time. Studies have also discovered that yo-yo dieting may increase cardiovascular risk factors (negatively affecting blood pressure, heart rate, and lipid levels)[34] [35] [36].

An ongoing cycle of weight loss and regain raises your weight range little by little. Your brain will play a significant role in determining this weight range: it will regulate your appetite[37] [38], metabolism, and energy storage to keep within the weight range, much like a thermostat regulating the temperature in your home.

WEIGHT SET POINT

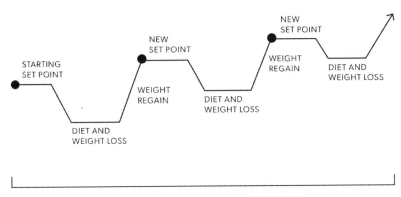

BODY WEIGHT FLUCTUATION OVER TIME

While some people do manage to maintain their weight loss over time, statistics indicate this is extremely rare[39]. One scientific review found that dieters experienced almost complete relapse after three to five years[40]. Are you beginning to question if your body has the capacity to get to your 'magic' number?

Throw out the scales!
You cannot make meaningful judgements about your weight on the basis of frequent weighing. Your weight will naturally fluctuate by between one to two kilograms each day or week[41]. Water retention is a common reason caused by high salt intake, dehydration, digestive problems or hormonal changes. Therefore, relying on a single figure can only lead to disappointment.

Weighing is a lose-lose behaviour. Weight loss may temporarily motivate you, especially at the start of a diet, but the risk is:

- If you gain weight, you feel bad – leading to bingeing/emotional eating
- If you lose weight, you may reward yourself with food

Weighing distracts you from your real feelings and teaches you to think how you **should** be feeling that day. *I've gained a pound therefore I feel depressed, a failure, guilty, ashamed... I've lost a pound therefore I feel happy, confident, successful.*

It also impacts your thoughts about your body from one day to the next depending on that very number, which we know fluctuates and is therefore unreliable. Suddenly you will feel fat because the number on the scales has increased from the previous day. When you think about it rationally, your body looks no different.

It's also worth pointing out that weight lost during dieting will give you an inaccurate representation of what is going on in your body. For example, a significant proportion of pounds shed at the start of a diet will consist of glycogen stores (your body's accessible energy source) and water – your fat stores will be unaffected. Glycogen and water will nearly always be replaced as soon as regular eating is restored[42].

So, my advice to you is to stop living by the numbers and get rid of your scales. When you no longer fixate on weight loss, you are far more likely to give your body what it needs. Engaging in healthful behaviours that make you feel good will allow your metabolism to heal and help you change your eating behaviours for good.

3. MANAGING YOUR MEALTIMES

Do you delay eating in an attempt to control your food intake, fearing that once you start eating, you won't be able to stop? Many individuals I work with express this concern. They've found that introducing a daily breakfast significantly reduces the chances of bingeing or overeating later in the day, a result supported by science[43].

By establishing a regular eating routine, your body will adapt to receiving energy at specific times, leading to a reduction in hunger and cravings[44] [45] [46]. This helps reduce the urge to seek out less helpful foods and will enable you to make more mindful decisions around food.

⚡ Action Step

EAT REGULAR MEALS
(BREAKFAST, LUNCH, DINNER)

Establish regular mealtimes with breakfast, lunch, and dinner. Don't overthink the food choices at first, consistency is key.

If you don't experience hunger early on in the day, consider starting with something small. Over time, as you establish a routine, you'll begin to notice a healthy morning hunger, preparing you for breakfast. In chapter 25 we'll be covering appetite retraining which will help you to feel more confident.

You may notice your anxiety levels rise at the thought of consuming more food than you think you currently eat, especially if you've been skipping meals or following intermittent fasting diets, but do trust in the process – bringing regularity to your eating is likely to reduce your overall food intake and help you to feel more in control.

☆ Client Story

Viv

Regular Mealtimes and Less Bingeing

Viv had struggled with her eating for almost 20 years. She hardly ate in the day – skipping breakfast and lunch and then snacking on pastries, crackers, and biscuits for the rest of the day. Sometimes, if given the opportunity and her family were out of the house, she would binge in the evening on food that had been stashed in her car. She felt terribly guilty and ashamed afterwards – vowing to start another diet the next day.

When I asked her if she noticed any hunger earlier on, she said that she did feel hungry but managed to 'get through' by drinking fizzy diet drinks from late morning onwards. When Viv started to eat three meals a day by gradually adding in one balanced meal at a time and slowly reduced her diet drink intake, she was no longer craving snack foods and felt satisfied and energised. This helped her to significantly reduce binge eating episodes as we began to work on other areas.

What to add in

The following chapters will assist you in constructing a balanced plate, managing your blood glucose (we'll explore why this is important in chapter 17), and adopting a more sustainable way to eat.

In chapter 16 you'll be introduced to the journal pages. These are designed for you to observe the connection between the food you eat and how you feel physically, such as your energy levels, digestion, and cravings. In addition, you'll come to recognise the triggers, thoughts, and feelings that are deeply entrenched with your eating behaviours.

4. PROTEIN POWER

I often see clients dealing with binge and emotional eating whose diets lack sufficient protein. Adding protein into each meal will help you in various ways. Firstly, protein helps to slow down the release of glucose into your bloodstream[47]. Unlike carbohydrates, which are broken down initially by enzymes in the saliva in your mouth, protein digestion begins in the stomach, gradually releasing food into the small intestine. This steady release allows for a gentle absorption of glucose, preventing huge, sudden spikes in blood glucose and excessive insulin release which would trigger a rapid drop in glucose and cravings. By pairing protein with carbohydrates, food will remain in your stomach for a prolonged period, helping to keep you fuller for longer, reducing cravings, and increasing satisfaction from your meal.

The satiating impact of protein is thought to be partially due to the *Protein Leverage Hypothesis*[48]. This suggests that humans will continue eating until they reach a target level of protein intake, regardless of the energy content of their food. Therefore, having inadequate protein in your diet could potentially lead to you overeating in an attempt to meet your body's required protein level.

Although protein is available in most foods, I am referring to the foods with a higher protein content listed below. The easiest way to consume a helpful amount of protein is by animal products (meat, poultry, fish, eggs, dairy). Though meeting protein needs is achievable for vegetarians or vegans, it may take a little more thought. Foods rich in plant-based protein such as lentils and beans tend to also contain a fair amount of complex carbohydrates, which lowers the overall protein content of that food.

Foods Rich in Protein: *White fish, oily fish, seafood, shellfish, poultry, meat, eggs, cheese, yoghurt, nuts, seeds, nut butters, tofu, tempeh, beans, lentils, chickpeas, hummus*

TIP: The same is true for snacks. Combining a handful of nuts, for example, with something sweet can help to curb the blood glucose spike of the sweet food

---

A Note on Meat

We are led to believe that meat is unhealthy due to its fat content. However, it is composed of essential amino acids vital for brain chemicals including serotonin (known as the happy hormone) and dopamine (associated with reward – extremely important when it comes to binge eating!). It provides important components for muscles, antibodies (proteins that help your immune system fight infection), and more. As a source of protein, meat helps to stabilise blood glucose and reduces cravings. Additionally, it's rich in essential micronutrients including calcium, iron, magnesium, zinc, potassium, and vitamins B3, B5, B6, and B12.

Meat isn't solely comprised of saturated fat; it also contains beneficial omega-3 fats and lacks unhealthy trans fats. (Further information on fats below.)

What if you are a vegetarian or vegan?

If you follow a vegetarian or vegan diet, consuming adequate protein requires careful planning and organisation. Legumes, such as chickpeas, borlotti, kidney, and cannellini beans, alongside lentils, provide plant-based protein options. However, these choices contain lower protein levels compared to animal sources and also contribute significantly to carbohydrate intake. Tofu, derived from soya beans, serves as an alternative protein for vegetarians, so opting for high-quality organic tofu is recommended. Tempeh, a traditional Asian food, is made from fermented whole soya beans and offers another vegetarian protein source.

Opting for processed plant-based options like veggie burgers might seem convenient, but the manufacturing process of these foods requires additives, including stabilisers, gums, thickeners, and highly processed protein extracts and may be nutritionally inferior to the animal products they replace[49].

Vegetarians and vegans often face greater nutrient deficiency challenges compared to those consuming meat, poultry, eggs, and fish[50] [51]. I will be covering how this can be managed with supplements in chapter 19.

TIP: Soak dried beans for 4-6 hours before cooking to deactivate the natural plant chemicals known as lectins that can cause digestive discomfort in some people.

TIP: Tofu and particularly tempeh can be bland – enhance the flavour using sauces, herbs, and spices – see additional resource section for seasoning information

TIP: Topping up your protein content with nuts and seeds is a straightforward way to include natural fats and a variety of micronutrients in addition to protein. These can be a fantastic addition to breakfast options like porridge oats or other cereal-based breakfasts. Mixed seeds also complement savoury dishes such as salads, avocado on toast, and soups. Try a combination of flax, chia, sesame, hemp, and pumpkin seeds and store them in a glass jar in the fridge to preserve their freshness.

This table provides an overview of the protein content of various plant and animal protein food sources*

Food Type	Protein per 100g	Protein in a standard portion	Contain Carbohydrate
Chicken fillet	24g	36g (150g portion)	x
Salmon fillet	25g	28.9g (115g portion)	x
Eggs large	13g	15g (2 large eggs)	x
Red split Lentils	9g	18g (200g portion)	14g
Cannellini beans	7g	14g (200g portion)	11g
Chickpeas	6g	12g (200g portion)	17g
Tofu	7g	11g (150g portion)	2g
Tempeh	17g	17g (100g portion)	11g
Quinoa	14g	7g (50g portion)	67g
Wholegrain rice	9g	4g (40g portion)	70g

*Amounts will vary slightly between food sources and figures provided have been rounded up.

⚡ Action Step

INCORPORATE PROTEIN INTO EACH MEAL

Consider ways to introduce protein into every meal, if it's not already part of your routine.

Example of sufficient protein consumption within a day:

2 x eggs

1 x tin of sardines

1 x tin of chickpeas

1 x mini pot of hummus

1 x breast of chicken

1 x 150g yoghurt pot

handful of nuts

This is in addition to smaller amounts of protein found in whole grains and vegetables

5. SMART CARBS

I've discussed how pairing any carbohydrate with protein can minimise the resulting blood glucose rise. However, opting for slow-releasing complex carbohydrates (refer to the table below) more frequently will amplify this effect.

Slow-releasing complex carbohydrates release their glucose more slowly than refined carbohydrate foods, providing a steady source of energy. Refined foods, such as white bread and other products made from refined white flour, lack fibre, causing a more rapid breakdown into glucose[52]. Refined carbohydrates also often lack essential nutrients that are key to blood glucose regulation, as these are stripped away during processing. There is a time and a place for refined carbs though. We don't need to banish them from our diets – instead consider switching to smarter carb options some of the time as you begin to build more balanced meals.

> **TIP:** Foods abundant in resistant starch help to lower blood glucose levels after eating. You can increase the resistant starch in starchy foods such as potatoes, pasta and rice by cooking and cooling them before eating. They can then be reheated or eaten cold. Beans, lentils, oats and barley are also sources of resistant starch.

Foods rich in slow-releasing complex carbohydrates:
Whole grains: wholegrain bread, pumpernickel, oatcakes, steel-cut oats, rolled oats, low-GL granola, beans, lentils, chickpeas, brown/wholegrain rice, quinoa, millet, buckwheat, brown rice noodles, wholegrain noodles, wholegrain pasta

Root vegetables: swede, beetroot, carrots, celeriac, parsnips, turnips, sweet potato, potatoes (baked, boiled with skin on) Peas, Jerusalem artichoke

Sweetcorn and corn on the cob, yams, cassava and plantain, pumpkin and squash

As a guide, vegetables with more than 5g of carbohydrate per 100g of weight can be considered starchy vegetables

A Note on Bread
A loaf of wholegrain bread is not always as it seems. As a rule, opt for bread with minimal processing and at least 6g per 100 g of fibre. The presence of fibre in the bread will help to slow the release of glucose into the bloodstream and curb cravings. Many highly processed breads, sold in supermarkets, contain limited amounts of fibre yet are still labelled as wholegrain. Pumpernickel-type breads tend to be higher in fibre and are therefore helpful for blood glucose regulation and your gut.

What about sourdough?

Authentic sourdough bread is a combination of wild yeast (naturally present in the air) and lactic bacteria (similar to those found in vinegar, cheese, and yoghurt). These elements, combined with a slow fermentation process, help to create bread that is not only easier to digest but also more nutritious. When it comes to bloating, many of my clients discover that they tolerate sourdough better than other bread varieties, so it's worth giving it a try. Be aware that several supermarkets are now producing 'imitation' sourdough which lacks these benefits. Genuine sourdough should **not** contain added yeast (check the ingredients list). It should be made from few ingredients, use a cultured flour starter, wholegrain flour, and undergo fermentation for a minimum of four to six hours.

⚡ Action Step

PRIORITISE SLOW-RELEASING COMPLEX CARBOHYDRATES

Replace some of the refined carbohydrates with slow-releasing carbohydrates within your meals. For example, consider substituting regular white bread with denser options like pumpernickel or seeded bread.

6. FUNCTIONAL FATS

There is a long-held misconception that we should be avoiding fat. Over the last 70 years, low-fat products have been marketed as the saviour of our health and weight, and weight and health have become very much intertwined within diet culture. The message from governments and the media is largely that the fat we eat gets stored as fat in the body and puts us at greater risk of heart disease. However, it is far more complex than that.

Part of the problem is that we use the same word for the fat within our body and the fat we eat. Many of the people I work with come to me with a profound fear of fats and are worried about weight gain or heart disease. However, the impact of fats on health and weight very much depends on the type of fats you are consuming or avoiding.

There are numerous reasons why fat is an essential component of our diet! It plays a fundamental role in absorbing fat-soluble vitamins (A, D, E and K) from our food. Omega-3 and omega-6 fats are 'essential' fats meaning that we must obtain them from our diet. While omega-6 fats are prevalent in Western diets, (such as foods containing vegetable oils) we especially need to focus on consuming omega-3 fats which are harder to come by.

Natural fats contribute to a feeling of satiety[53] in part because they trigger the release of hormones that help us to feel satisfied after eating.

There are three natural fats: saturated, monounsaturated and polyunsaturated. All fat-containing foods contain a combination of these. You may be familiar with trans fats (industrially produced trans-fatty acids). While trace amounts of these fats occur naturally in some wholefoods, it is processed foods that are abundant in trans fats and, importantly, these types of fats are detrimental to health.

A Note on the Types of Fats

Saturated fats are present in animal-based foods such as meat and dairy, as well as in coconut oil. Despite the widespread belief that saturated fat consumption is associated with cardiovascular risks and mortality, there is insufficient conclusive evidence to substantiate this[54] [55]. These fats, found naturally in nutrient-rich foods, can be safely included in a balanced diet in moderation.

Monounsaturated fats are associated with the traditional Mediterranean diet – particularly olive oil – and populations that eat a lot of these fats, like the people of Greece and Italy, have some of the lowest rates of heart disease in the world[56]. Avocados, often dismissed as too calorific, are also high in monounsaturated fats (and rich in vitamin E).

Polyunsaturated fats include **omega-3 and omega-6 essential fats**. They cannot be made in the body and therefore must be eaten as part of your diet (or taken as a supplement). Omega-3-rich foods include oily fish, such as salmon, nuts, and seeds.

These fats have many roles in the body. Sufficient levels have implications for cell membranes, hormones (they regulate insulin function), managing inflammation and immunity, mood and memory. In fact, your brain's dry weight consists of 60% fat, and omega-3 fats are critical for communication between brain cells. That's why consumption of oily fish (an important source of omega-3) is linked with better brain function[57].

Monounsaturated fats and omega-3 fats are the most efficient at stimulating the release of the satiety hormone leptin[58] which tells us when it's time to stop eating.

Trans fats are far less efficient at stimulating the release of leptin. We are less likely to feel satisfied after eating foods that contain trans fats and are more likely to continue to eat, even if we are full.

Natural Fats:
Olive oil, avocado oil, flaxseed oil, walnut oil, ghee, coconut oil, coconut cream, coconut yoghurt, almonds, macadamia nut, nut butters, grass-fed butter, flaxseeds, chia seeds, pumpkin seeds, sesame seeds, tahini, avocado, olives, guacamole

⚡ Action Step

INCLUDE A VARIETY OF NATURAL FATS IN YOUR DIET

Consider where you can introduce natural fats into your meals (for example adding nuts and seeds to your breakfast or salads) and reducing the consumption of processed foods containing trans fat.

7. FIBRE FIX

Fibre consists of insoluble fibre, which doesn't dissolve in water, such as wholewheat flour, bran, and vegetables, and water-dissolving soluble fibre, for instance oats and legumes.

Fibre is especially helpful for slowing down the release of glucose from your food into your bloodstream, helping you to feel more satiated[59] [60]. This is where things can seem a little confusing. Fibre is found in starchy vegetables, whole grains, legumes (beans and lentils), nuts and seeds, and non-starchy vegetables. Since we have already covered all but the latter, let's take a look at the non-starchy vegetable group. These are generally vegetables that grow above ground and come in a variety of colours, shapes, and sizes!

> **Non-Starchy Vegetables – all the colours of the rainbow:**
> *Butternut squash, courgettes, asparagus, cucumber, peppers, aubergines, tomatoes, watercress, spinach, cabbage, cauliflower, broccoli, kale, green beans, runner beans, red cabbage, savoy cabbage, Brussel sprouts, onions, leeks, spring onions, red onions, brown onions, okra, rocket, lettuce*

⚡ **Action Step**

INCORPORATE A VARIETY OF NON-STARCHY VEGETABLES INTO YOUR DIET

Introduce a diverse selection of non-starchy vegetables into your meals wherever possible. Challenge yourself to consume vegetables from all colour groups within a week, including yellow/orange, greens, white, blue/purple, and pink/red (fruit can be included in this too).

8. BALANCING YOUR PLATE

The *Balanced Plate* is a simple and effective way to ensure you are eating all the macronutrients you need without weighing and measuring your food. This will help to keep you satiated and energised. However, it's important to avoid fixating on the idea that every meal should strictly follow the same proportions; instead view this as a helpful starting point. When composing your meals use the *Balanced Plate* as a guide while also considering factors such as eating out, available ingredients, and time constraints. **Please do not treat the *Balanced Plate* as a dieting food rule.**

> **TIP:** The Balanced Plate will look slightly different for vegetarians and vegans. In this case, the plant-based protein source should occupy more than a quarter of the plate to allow for the carbohydrates present in the food contributing to a proportion of the meal's total carbohydrate content.

THE BALANCED PLATE

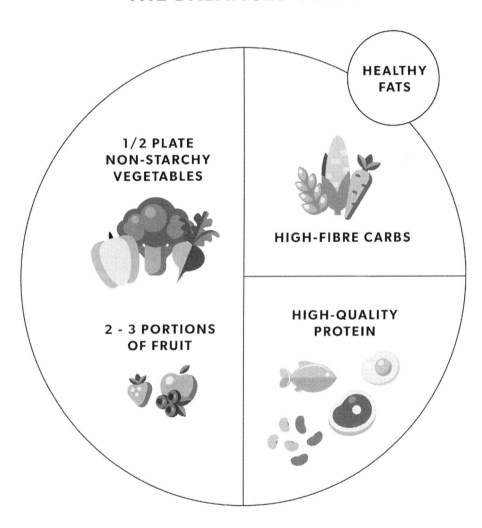

Most foods fall into multiple categories. The table below summarises the elements of the *Balanced Plate*.

Protein	Natural Fats	Starchy Carbohydrates*	Non-Starchy Vegetables and Fruit
White fish, oily fish, seafood, shellfish, poultry, meat, eggs, cheese, yoghurt, nuts, seeds, nut butters, tofu, tempeh, beans, lentils, chickpeas, hummus	Olive oil, avocado oil, flaxseed oil, walnut oil, ghee, coconut oil, coconut cream, coconut yoghurt, almonds, macadamia nut, nut butters, grass-fed butter, flaxseeds, chia seeds, pumpkin seeds, sesame seeds, tahini, avocado, olives, guacamole	Whole grains: wholegrain bread, pumpernickel, oatcakes, steel-cut oats, rolled oats, low-GL granola, beans, lentils, chickpeas, brown/wholegrain rice, quinoa, millet, buckwheat, brown rice noodles, wholegrain noodles, wholegrain pasta Root vegetables: swede, beetroot, carrots, celeriac, parsnips, turnips, sweet potato Other vegetables: peas, Jerusalem artichoke, potatoes (baked, boiled with skin on), sweetcorn and corn on the cob, yams, cassava, plantain, pumpkin, squash *As a guide, vegetables with more than 5g of carbohydrate per 100g of weight are in the starchy carb category	Butternut squash, courgettes, asparagus, cucumber, peppers, aubergines, tomatoes, watercress, spinach, cabbage, cauliflower, broccoli, kale, green beans, runner beans, red cabbage, savoy cabbage, Brussel sprouts, onions, leeks, spring onions, red onions, brown onions, okra, rocket, lettuce, berries, apples, pears, melon, nectarine, citrus fruit

If you're having difficulty identifying what a balanced meal might consist of, use the meal-planning tool provided below. Begin by listing all your preferred meals and snacks, noting what you eat most frequently, and then complete each section accordingly. If you are missing any components, consider what you could add in to that meal or snack and adjust the proportions to make it more complete.

A printable template of the meal-planning tool can be downloaded at:
https://marcellerosenutrition.co.uk/book-resources

Meal	Protein	Fats	Starchy carbohydrate	Non-starchy vegetables/ fruit	Fibre
Porridge oats with whole milk, grated apple, walnuts, flax seeds, pumpkin seeds + cinnamon	Whole milk, walnuts, flax seeds, pumpkin seeds	Whole milk, walnuts, flax seeds, pumpkin seeds	Porridge oats	Grated apple	Porridge oats, walnuts, flax seeds, grated apple
Large bowl of home-made minestrone soup containing borlotti beans, tomato, onion, carrots, kale, celery, and olive oil with wholegrain sourdough toast	Borlotti beans	Olive oil	Wholegrain sourdough toast, borlotti beans, carrots	Tomato, onion, kale, celery	Borlotti beans, tomato, onion, carrots, kale, celery, wholegrain sourdough toast
Roasted salmon with miso marinade, brown rice, and stir-fried broccoli, onion, mushrooms, and cashew nuts	Salmon, cashew nuts, miso	Salmon, cashew nuts	Brown rice, miso	Broccoli, onion, mushrooms	Brown rice broccoli, onion, mushrooms, cashew nuts

TIP: Don't attempt to balance all three meals at once, start with one meal at a time. Consider which meal – breakfast, lunch, or dinner – would be the most manageable to begin with. See chapters 9-11 for guidance on this.

A Note on the Structure & Texture of Your Food

Whilst using the *Balanced Plate* helps you to take into account the different components of your meals, there are also the structure and texture of individual foods to consider.

Each food consists of a complex structure – known as the food matrix[61]. This will influence the food's specific nutritional properties, texture, taste, and quality. Food processing alters this matrix structure. For instance, milling whole grains to produce refined grains (such as white flour and white rice) extracts the bran and germ, thereby removing the fibre and micronutrient content, while also affecting how the body digests and absorbs these foods.

The texture of food can significantly impact the speed at which you eat and the amount you consume. When food is hard, dry, chewy, or crispy it requires more chewing, which slows down the eating process. This increased chewing time allows your body more time to receive satiety signals, potentially leading to feeling satisfied sooner[62].

Research indicates that people tend to eat more when food is in a liquid or very smooth form. In fact, people consume about 30% more of a liquid food compared to a semi-solid food, even if both taste the same and have the same amount of calories and nutrients.[63]

Consider the structure of oats for instance[64]:

Steel-cut oats are whole oat groats that have been chopped into smaller pieces. They retain more of the oat's natural structure, leading to slower digestion. As a result, they have less impact on blood glucose compared to more processed forms of oats. Slower digestion also provides a more sustained release of energy, keeping you fuller for longer.

Rolled oats, on the other hand, are oat groats that have been steamed and then flattened into flakes reducing their cooking time in comparison to steel-cut oats. The structure of rolled oats allow digestive enzymes in the gut to access the starches more easily causing a more pronounced effect on blood glucose levels than steel-cut oats.

Instant oatmeal undergoes further processing where the oat flakes are finely ground into a powder. Typically pre-cooked, flavoured, and packaged for quick preparation, the finer texture allows for rapid digestion and absorption of carbohydrates, resulting in sharper blood glucose spikes.

Different cooking and preparation methods also alter the texture of food. For example, boiling vegetables until they are soft versus lightly steaming them, or eating whole fruit instead of blending it into a smoothie, can change the texture and, consequently, how quickly you feel satiated when eating these foods.

9. A NUTRITIOUS START: A FOCUS ON BREAKFAST

As mentioned earlier, incorporating a balanced breakfast can make a significant difference to your hunger and cravings later in the day, so I recommend to start by focusing on this meal. Begin by introducing just one or two ideas (such as those included below) and alternate them. Refer to the *Balanced Plate* as a reminder of what key components to include in your meal. When you become comfortable with your initial breakfast ideas you can begin to introduce new options.

Here are a few suggestions:

- Overnight oats with grated apple, chia seeds, cinnamon, and walnuts
- Full-fat natural yogurt with berries, pumpkin and flax seeds, and pecan nuts
- Scrambled eggs with half an avocado, tomatoes, wilted spinach, and a slice of rye bread

---

Bonus Resource

For more ideas, go to https://marcellerosenutrition.co.uk/book-resouces to download my selection of delicious, balanced breakfast, lunch, dinner and snack recipes.

⚡ Action Step

FOCUS ON BREAKFASTS

Pick two new breakfast choices to start with or assess what to add to current breakfast choices to ensure they are balanced.

If you are already confident with your breakfast choices, skip to the next step.

10. NIGHT-TIME NOURISHMENT: A FOCUS ON DINNER

Next, turn your attention to your evening meals. There may be meals you currently make that can be tweaked to create a balanced dinner.

For instance, consider a dish like pasta with tomato sauce – it would be helpful to increase fibre content and introduce protein. You might like to include a side salad to increase fibre and consider incorporating lentils, minced meat, or tuna to the pasta sauce, for added protein. You can then adjust the pasta portion.

You could also begin with a few simply assembled meals.

Here are a few suggestions:

- Roast chicken breast, roast sweet potato, and mixed salad
- Chicken/tofu/prawn stir-fry with mangetout, shredded cabbage, red pepper, broccoli, and onion with brown rice
- Grilled salmon, quinoa, and roasted vegetables

For more ideas, go to https://marcellerosenutrition.co.uk/book-resources to download my selection of delicious, balanced breakfast, lunch, dinner and snack recipes.

⚡ **Action Step**

FOCUS ON EVENING MEALS

Think of an existing meal you enjoy and consider if and how it can be adjusted using the *Balanced Plate* as a guideline.

---

11. MIDDAY MEALS: A FOCUS ON LUNCH

When you feel confident with your evening meals and breakfast, shift your attention to your lunchtime meals. This could be more challenging if you are not at home during the day. It's totally fine if you buy your lunch while you're out, but take a moment to consider if it meets your nutritional needs. If you buy the same old sandwich every day, then perhaps it's time to mix things up. Experiment with preparing a balanced packed lunch a few days a week. It's not advisable to attempt this every day at first, in order to keep it manageable.

Leftovers from a previous evening meal can make an excellent packed lunch. Purchase some good containers; opt for metal or glass containers over plastics (old jam jars work well as airtight containers, especially for preparing overnight oats for breakfast). Insulated flask-type containers are handy for winter, especially for soups that can be heated before leaving home, so you can still enjoy a hot meal if there are no facilities at work. Allow for leftovers in your meal planning.

Below are a few suggestions:

- Tinned sardines or mackerel mashed on rye bread with sliced cucumber, with a simple side salad
- Roast chicken leftovers added to a mixed salad
- Chunky minestrone soup made with borlotti beans and a variety of vegetables with a few oatcakes

For more ideas, go to https://marcellerosenutrition.co.uk/book-resources to download my selection of delicious, balanced, meal and snack recipes.

⚡ Action Step

A FOCUS ON LUNCH

Whether you're having lunch at work or at home, it's important to be prepared with options readily available for quick assembly or leftovers that are easily prepped for a quick, convenient meal. If you opt to buy lunch while out, apply the *Balanced Plate* guidelines to help you select your meal.

Ideas for buying your lunch out:

- Think chunky vegetable soups containing protein such as chicken, beans or lentils.
- Salads with protein such as quinoa and feta, tuna Niçois, beans, lentils, nuts and seeds.
- Buy vegetable-based salad and add your own protein such as ready-cooked salmon, smoked salmon, tinned sardines, smoked mackerel, tuna, roast chicken, hard-boiled egg and cottage cheese.
- Wholemeal wraps made with salad and a protein such as hummus, tuna, chicken, halloumi, and feta.

12. PLANNING YOUR MEALTIMES

Having to think on the hoof about your next meal whilst juggling other responsibilities can be stressful, and staying organised may often fall to the bottom of your priority list. However, by creating a simple plan, you can alleviate the overwhelm associated with food decisions. The emphasis here is on developing skills and building autonomy to regain a sense of control and not on having the perfect meal plan or diet.

Without a plan, it becomes a matter of chance whether you'll have the necessary food stocked in your kitchen. Similarly, without scheduling your time, you're more likely to find excuses for missing breakfasts or being unprepared for lunch.

If you're committed to changing your eating habits, allocating a small amount of time for planning will help you to structure your mealtimes, work towards a more balanced diet, and reduce your chances of gravitating towards less helpful foods.

⚡ Action Step

PLAN YOUR MEALS

Here's how to get started:

1. Schedule in time to meal plan and do your shop, whether online or in person. Think about when a suitable time for this would be. Planning a week in advance may feel too overwhelming at first, so consider how many days in advance you will plan for.

2. Make a plan for your evening meals first, as this is often the most challenging meal to get organised. It is likely to feel too overwhelming if you try to plan all your meals within a day.

3. Create a master list by brainstorming all the evening meals cooked in the past that you enjoyed or worked well for you and your family. This will provide an easy and quick reference to help you create your meal plan. Whenever you try a new meal and consider it a success, add it to your master list. Organise this list into categories such as chicken, fish, meat, vegetarian, and so on, and keep it in an easily accessible place!

4. Pinpoint three staple, go-to evening meals, something quick and easy that you always have the necessary ingredients for. This is useful for when you are time-poor or just don't feel like doing anything different.

5. Use my weekly meal planner below to plan your evening meals. You can even add the ingredients to your shopping list as you go. Use your master list and have a look at my recipe selection for some ideas (both the weekly meal planner and recipe selection are available at https://marcellerosenutrition.co.uk/book-resources). I would only recommend introducing one new recipe idea in a week unless it's something that doesn't faze you.

6. Leftovers save time and energy! Make double the amount to use for lunch or your dinner the next day. For example, repurpose your roast chicken or grilled salmon in a salad the following day for lunch. You can also make extra to freeze into portions. Stews, soups, bolognaise, chilli, lasagna, and the like work well for this.

7. Check your schedule for the week. If you have activities in the evening, or you are working late, perhaps that's when leftovers or defrosting one of your pre-prepared meals will come in handy. A slow cooker meal can also be a lifesaver where you can start cooking it the night before. Meals don't have to be overcomplicated – have some quick, easy-to-assemble plate ideas up your sleeve and ensure you have the right ingredients available.

8. Whilst cooking and already in the kitchen, use this time to prep some ingredients for the next few days, for example chopping veg, cooking grains or chicken to keep in the fridge.

9. When you have mastered planning your evening meals, you can try planning for breakfast and lunch. Even if they are easier meals, planning them ensures you have the ingredients you need and allows you time to prepare. For example, overnight oats can be prepared the night before, for breakfast the following morning.

WEEKLY MEAL PLANNER

WHAT TO EAT	SHOPPING LIST
M	
T	
W	
T	
F	
S	
S	

How to make simple meals more exciting

Use herbs and spices to enhance the natural flavours of the food, adding a variety of colour and wonderful aromas. In addition to making meals tastier, herbs and spices are rich in antioxidants, minerals, and vitamins. As you'll discover in chapter 22, herbs and spices help to expand the diversity of your food intake, required by your gut bacteria, so it's win-win. Check out my herbs and spices in the additional resource section at the end of the book to help with this.

Sauces and dressings can also add an extra dimension to a simple meal. Opt for making your own rather than using store-bought options which often contain artificial additives, sweeteners, and sugars. Simple ideas for creating your own sauces and dressings can be found in the additional resource section at the back of the book.

> **TIP:** Pre-mince garlic and ginger, freeze in an ice cube tray and empty into a container to store in the freezer to use when needed. Alternatively, you can buy 'lazy' garlic and ginger in a jar.

> **TIP:** Try different spice blends such as Baharat, jerk, Creole. These can be added to fish or chicken with some oil as a marinade.

☆ Client Story

Faye

Breaking Free from Restriction, Hunger and Cravings

I met Faye when she was 39. She had been yo-yo dieting since the age of 16. She sought my help for her challenges with emotional eating and a sense of complete loss of control around food. By now, she felt extremely confused about what foods to eat having experimented with various diets that imposed different rules and restrictions.

Faye never felt satisfied after eating and her constant preoccupation with food became apparent as we reviewed her journal together. It became clear that Faye's eating was chaotic, as she avoided regular meals and largely excluded carbohydrates and fats from her diet in an attempt to shed weight. This pattern led to a nightly cycle of grazing on sugary snacks ranging from cereal to biscuits and chocolate, which then triggered feelings of anxiety, distress, and guilt.

During our time working together, Faye gradually reintroduced the missing carbohydrates and fats back into her meals. She was now able to include home-made dressings with olive oil and tahini, avocado, nuts, seeds, and various whole grains within her mealtimes.

This shift had a significant impact, not only on her constant hunger but also changed her evening eating behaviour. She no longer felt the need to snack every night, which had an incredible impact on other aspects of her life. She was now able to enjoy sharing meals and connecting with others and no longer felt the need to go to bed straight after dinner, just to escape the food! Faye learned, over time, to give herself permission to eat previously forbidden snacks too, creating a sense of freedom and clarity in her relationship with food.

13. INTENTIONAL SNACKS

It's a common belief that pleasurable foods rich in sugar, fat, and refined carbohydrates must be completely eradicated from your diet. It's likely you experience feelings of guilt and remorse when eating these foods. However, adopting a restrictive mindset can be counterproductive, making you more susceptible to bingeing or feeling out of control when exposed to them.

I understand that it might take some time to become comfortable with embracing all foods as part of your diet, so don't try to do everything at once. However, it can be helpful to try a small portion of your 'forbidden' food after lunch rather than as a snack, to help keep your blood glucose levels in check. If you do feel like eating it at snack time, pair it up with a protein-containing option to prevent further cravings and keep checking in with your appetite using the hunger scale. (We will be covering this in chapter 25.)

You might think it's logical to delay eating as much as you can or criticise yourself for feeling hungry before your scheduled mealtime, however, it is critical to avoid waiting until you are excessively hungry. When you reach a level of about 70% hunger, I recommend you *mindfully* choose to have a snack, but eat it slowly. Ideally, only eat a snack when you genuinely experience hunger, but if you don't, just observe without judgement why you may have turned to food. (We will explore this topic further in chapter 16.)

How do you know if you're experiencing a craving and not true hunger?

You are likely to feel an uncontrollable urgency to eat a **specific** food if it's a craving. If it's genuine hunger, the snack is usually interchangeable with other foods. However, the lines become blurred because being over hungry can result in cravings too. Remember that cravings can also rage when your blood glucose levels are out of balance.

Always have some backup snack options available and try to include some protein where possible.

Snack Ideas
- Nuts (e.g. almonds, walnuts, macadamias, pine nuts)
- Nuts with a few pieces of dark chocolate
- Nuts and piece of fruit
- Seeds (e.g. pumpkin, sunflower)
- Hard-boiled eggs with spinach
- Banana with a handful of almonds
- A handful of walnuts with a few pieces of dark chocolate and a palmful of raspberries/blueberries
- Mashed avocado on sourdough sprinkled with chia seeds
- Mackerel pâté on a slice of rye bread with cucumber
- Vegetable sticks with hummus/tahini
- Sliced apple with nut butter
- Oatcakes/seed crackers with nut/seed butter/hummus
- Cottage cheese and tomato on oatcakes
- Coconut chips
- Kale chips
- Sourdough bread/rye bread with avocado and seeds sprinkled on top
- Full-fat natural yoghurt with berries and seeds
- Edamame (soya beans)
- Roasted seaweed

- Seed crackers
- Protein bars/balls
- A handful of roasted chickpeas
- Large handful of cherry tomatoes and 5-8 cubes of feta
- Handful of home-made trail mix (your own mix of: seeds, nuts, toasted coconut strips, cocoa nibs, or a small amount of dark chocolate chopped, home-made popcorn, etc.)

⚡ Action Step

SNACK WITH INTENTION

Here's how to make the most of snacks to alleviate hunger:

Be prepared with snack options in advance and have them readily available for when needed.

Don't wait until you become over hungry before eating.

Choose nutrient-dense options – opt for snacks that are rich in nutrients and provide sustained energy. Where possible, try a combination of protein, healthy fats, and complex carbohydrates (refer back to the *Balanced Plate*).

14. DRINK RETHINK?

What and how much you drink can impact blood glucose levels and may influence your eating. Hydrating yourself is important for all aspects of health, and lack of sufficient fluids can impact your energy and concentration and can be mistaken for hunger.

How to know if you are properly hydrated?
Check your urine – it should be fairly clear – if it is dark yellow, it could be a sign you need to drink more water[65]. If you feel fatigued, dizzy, confused, have a headache, or find concentrating difficult, these are signs you could be dehydrated. Perhaps you have bad breath or a dry mouth, lips, or skin? Constipation is another sign of dehydration, though there could be a number of reasons why you might experience this.

How much water do you need to drink?

Water intake recommendations will vary according to the season, your body weight, level of activity, and specific health conditions[66]. About 1.5-2 litres a day is a general recommendation, but it will depend on how much physical activity you do and your individual needs – tune into what feels right for you and keep an eye on your urine colour!

Herbals teas, smoothies, and soups can all count towards your hydration too, due to the water content in veggies.

While it is important to listen to your body, you want to get ahead of feeling thirsty as, by this time, it is likely that you are already dehydrated.

Ideas to Increase Water Intake:

- Start the day with warm water with a slice of lemon, lime, or ginger. This can help with digestion or if you feel nauseous in the morning
- Keep a water bottle with you at your desk and take it with you wherever you go
- Add herbs or fruit such as fresh mint, basil, berries, sliced cucumber, or citrus fruit to a jug of water to add a subtle refreshing flavour
- Enjoy your favourite herbal tea hot or as an iced drink. Brew the tea, leave to cool in fridge and add ice. A number of brands that are now available in supermarkets produce some lovely herbal blends.

Diet Drinks

Diet drinks may seem like a better choice, but the artificial sweeteners in them are about as helpful for blood glucose regulation as the full sugar varieties, so it's best to limit consumption of these. (More on this in chapter 18.)

What about Juice?

The fibre in whole fruit helps to slow down the absorption of natural sugars present in fruit, when it is eaten in its whole, raw state. Fruit juice, however, is produced by separating the liquid from the fibre, and so natural sugars are absorbed more quickly, leading to blood glucose spikes[67].

Vegetable juices may also quickly elevate blood glucose, so it's worth limiting intake of all juices. Go for freshly made, when you do consume it, as the longer the juice is exposed to light and oxygen, the fewer nutrients are available.

Remember, the best way to access the vitamins, minerals, and antioxidants in fruit is to have it in its whole, raw state; ideally pairing it with some protein – for example, an apple with a handful of nuts.

Caffeine

While coffee can enhance alertness, productivity, and motivation for some, it may lead others to feel anxious, jittery, and unable to focus[68]. Therefore, reducing coffee consumption needs to be a personal decision, depending on how it affects you.

Caffeine acts as a stimulant, potentially increasing stress hormones[69], which can affect your mood, energy levels, and sleep patterns. Additionally, it can disrupt your insulin response, resulting in roller-coasting highs and lows – leaving you feeling exhausted.

Caffeine affects sleep by blocking adenosine, a natural compound in the brain that signals the need for relaxation[70]. Adenosine promotes relaxation by decreasing your brain activity and inducing drowsiness. Simultaneously, caffeine promotes alertness by stimulating the release of stimulating brain chemicals.

If you suspect that caffeine is negatively impacting you, it's advisable to gradually decrease consumption rather than going 'cold turkey'. Transitioning to half cups of coffee initially can be a helpful approach.

It's also worth considering the connection between needing a snack each time you drink a cup of coffee (or tea). If you've noticed this pattern, think about how much you genuinely enjoy your coffee or tea without the associated snacking.

And Alcohol?

Drinking alcohol, particularly in larger quantities, might help you to fall asleep quickly; however, it will disrupt your sleep cycle throughout the night[71]. Alcohol reduces the amount of REM sleep[72], which is essential for mental restoration, leaving you feeling unrefreshed the following morning. (Discover more about the effects of inadequate sleep on your eating habits in chapter 24.)

The other problem with alcohol is that it creates disinhibition and is likely to affect your decision-making when it comes to food. Bingeing on alcohol is often a precursor to bingeing on food and even a small tipple may distract you from being mindful about your eating[73]. It's also worth noting that the liver will always prioritise the breakdown of alcohol over food, hence slowing down your metabolism and reducing its energy burning capacity!

If you occasionally drink alcohol, try opting for clear spirits; for example, vodka, soda water, and lime (avoiding the usual mixers), as they contain no carbohydrates and therefore have a reduced impact on blood glucose levels. Though dryer wines contain less sugar, beer and wine in general may present more challenges when it comes to your cravings.

Using Drinks to Curb Your Hunger?

Are you using water, fizzy drinks/soda, or coffee to replace food?

Ultimately, this approach won't leave you feeling satisfied, and you'll be more inclined to eat larger amounts of food later in the day or experience a binge-eating episode. We will be exploring the importance of recognising your hunger cues and responding to them accordingly, in chapter 25.

⚡ Action Step

RETHINK YOUR DRINKS

Keep track of your hydration levels and substitute unhelpful drinks with water, herbal teas, or infused water. Replace drinks that may destabilise your blood glucose levels, cause dehydration, or exacerbate cravings. Avoid drinking as a means to suppress hunger – this may or may not be intentional. If you are hungry you must eat.

Shortly, you'll discover the journal to assist you with this.

Important note: Give yourself permission to be flexible and don't beat yourself up for deviations. It's totally okay to enjoy meals out with friends and family or enjoy fun foods. Remember, this is not a diet but about building new skills to help you care for yourself in the most sustainable way possible.

15. BUT I DON'T HAVE TIME

Not having time is a common story we tell ourselves. If this resonates with you, let me assure you that it is possible to make time for what truly matters in your life. If you're reading this with a "yes, but..." mindset, take a look at how you are spending your time. How do you feel about how you are spending your time? Are you in control of your time? If you looked back over your life, would you be happy with the way you had spent your time? This really could be life-changing. To help you become more aware of how you spend time, try the activity below.

⚡ Action Step

THE DAILY TIME PLANNER

Over the coming week, use the Daily Time Planner below to record everything you do in the time slots provided. This exercise can help to uncover the real reason behind why you don't think you have time for what you want to do. It's not uncommon, for instance, to realise that you're spending over 10 hours a week aimlessly scrolling on social media.

(A printable version of the Daily Time Planner is available to download at https://marcellerosenutrition.co.uk/book-resources)

Where are you losing time or being inefficient with it? What is the cost of spending your time like this? Does it make it impossible to make changes with your eating? Are the coffee shop bills piling up because you haven't made time to make breakfast at home? It's often remarkable how much time you can reclaim and work towards creating the life that you want.

	Monday	Tuesday	Wednesday
7-8			
8-9			
9-10			
10-11			
11-12			
12-13			
13-14			
14-15			
15-16			
16-17			
17-18			
18-19			
19-20			
20-21			
21-22			
22-23			
23-24			

Thursday	Friday	Saturday	Sunday

16. USING THE JOURNAL

Many people are oblivious to what else is happening in the context of their eating habits. Most people who binge-eat are doing so in a 'trance-like' state. Some people hugely underestimate what they eat. Others can build a catastrophic picture in their mind because they may have broken a self-imposed food rule.

The journal acts like a window into your mind. It's a behavioural tool enabling you to become your own coach by observing what you are doing rather than just doing it. It fosters self-awareness of your behaviour patterns, habits thoughts, and emotions, helping you to identify the triggers to your unwanted behaviour. With time, you'll acquire problem-solving techniques to handle situations differently in the future.

Furthermore, given your individual health history, genetics, and biochemistry, your body will react in its own way to different foods and meals. The journal can be used to help identify which foods bring you the most satisfaction, help to control cravings, and help you to feel good in your body. Don't forget to consider what you genuinely enjoy eating too!

⚡ **Action Step**

USING THE JOURNAL

Use the *journal pages* provided below to observe your eating habits without judgement. It's essential to remember that the journal serves as a tool for self-discovery, reflection, and personal growth, rather than amplifying your inner critical voice.

You can download a printable version of the journal at https://marcellerosenutrition.co.uk/book-resources)

Here's how to begin:

Note down what and when you are eating (and drinking)

Where you are, with whom, and if you are doing something else during your meals (e.g. watching TV)

Acknowledge any wins, no matter how small, such as adding in breakfast or being prepared with snacks

Record any instances of binge or emotional eating and label these as a *learning experience*. This is an important part of the process from which you can learn and develop problem-solving strategies to do something differently next time

Identify any situations that trigger a binge or attempts to restrain

As you progress through the book, you'll begin to expand your journal entries to include observations on your appetite, thought patterns, and emotional triggers

Food Journal

Date:

	Food & drink	Appetite before & after 1-10	Where, with who?	Energy, stress, boredom, thoughts & feelings	Learing experience? Any wins?
Breakfast					
Snacks					
Lunch					
Snacks					
Dinner					
Snacks					

Action Plan Summary

Focus on one action step at a time. Take your time to ensure you feel confident with each step before proceeding to the next one.

Action	What will this help with?	Duration	Chapter reference	Notes
Establish regular mealtimes	Stabilising blood glucose, reducing cravings and hunger	Ongoing	3	
A focus on breakfasts	Get the day off to a good start, preventing cravings and hunger later in the day	Ongoing	9 Refer to chapters 4-8 to assist you with this	
A focus on evening meals	Stabilising blood glucose, reducing cravings and hunger, building on a diverse balanced diet	Ongoing	10 Refer to chapters 4-8 to assist you with this	
A focus on lunch	Reducing dietary chaos. Helping to prevent binge or grazing episodes later in the day	Ongoing	11 Refer to chapters 4-8 to assist you with this	
Plan your meals	Simple meal planning will help support the above and reduce stress around food, reduce the likelihood of cravings, binges, and emotional eating episodes	Ongoing	12	
Be prepared with helpful snack options	It's important to avoid becoming over hungry and being prepared with a helpful snack will reduce the chances of binge or compulsive eating	Ongoing	13	

Action	What will this help with?	Duration	Chapter reference	Notes
A focus on drinks	Remain hydrated, stabilising blood glucose, reducing cravings and hunger, reducing dietary chaos	Ongoing	14	
Daily Time Planner	Optional step if you find it challenging to allocate time to do things for yourself	One-off exercise but can be repeated periodically if required	15	
Using the Journal	Begin to develop an understanding of your eating behaviour and patterns	Ongoing	16	

pillar two: balance

Within this section of the book, you will learn how to balance the key physical systems that influence your appetite and cravings, and shape your eating patterns. You'll discover how your brain chemicals, hormones, gut microbiome, circadian rhythm (and more) impact your eating behaviours and how to support them within your body. Armed with these insights and strategies, you'll gain a greater sense of control over your cravings, paving the way for a more mindful and balanced approach to eating.

17. PHYSICAL CRAVINGS

Not all cravings are biological; there are numerous reasons why we might turn to food to soothe us. Nonetheless, it's critical to address the underlying physiological factors that contribute to these cravings as part of the groundwork.

As outlined in the first chapter, engaging in food restriction brings about physiological changes in the body. As a result of dieting, your body will release more hunger hormones which tell your brain it's time to eat, and less of the hormones that signal the feeling of satiation. This isn't you being weak-willed, lazy, or greedy but your body's internal mechanism at work.

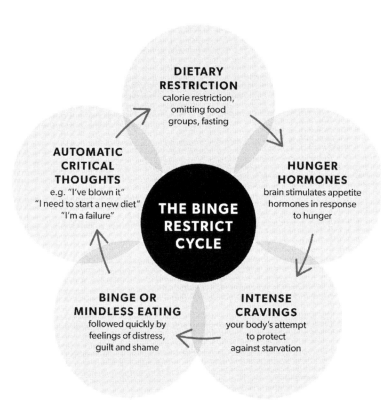

DIETARY RESTRICTION
calorie restriction, omitting food groups, fasting

HUNGER HORMONES
brain stimulates appetite hormones in response to hunger

INTENSE CRAVINGS
your body's attempt to protect against starvation

BINGE OR MINDLESS EATING
followed quickly by feelings of distress, guilt and shame

AUTOMATIC CRITICAL THOUGHTS
e.g. "I've blown it" "I need to start a new diet" "I'm a failure"

THE BINGE RESTRICT CYCLE

Very often this cycle will persist because further restriction has taken place in an attempt to compensate for calories consumed. This is especially common following an episode of perceived overeating or consumption of 'forbidden' foods, and so, the cycle continues. You might believe that avoiding food for as long as possible will either help you to lose weight or control your eating in some way, but in fact, this will have the opposite outcome[74].

The Glucose Connection

The brain and body need glucose as a primary source of energy[75], with the brain alone consuming one third of your energy requirements. It is constantly striving to maintain a steady supply of glucose at all times. However, when glucose sensors in the brain detect low levels, stored glucose is released into the bloodstream which will lead you to experience the urge to search for food.

It is natural for your blood glucose levels to rise each time you eat. Whether that's by a little or a lot depends partly on what the meal consisted of. Refined carbohydrates and sugars (such as pastries, biscuits, cakes, and plain white bread) cause a steeper spike in glucose than complex carbohydrates[76] (which include whole grains such as oats, brown rice, buckwheat, barley, etc.)

When your blood glucose is high, you won't really feel it, but the higher the blood glucose, the more this triggers the release of the hormone insulin. This high insulin activity will cause your glucose level to plummet. When it drops too low, you may experience energy slumps, difficulty focusing, irritability, hunger, and cravings[77]. Extended periods without eating can also lead to a drop in blood glucose, prompting the brain to send out signals that the body needs to replenish its energy source.

It is easy to become stuck in a continuous cycle where blood glucose levels rise sharply to a peak and then crash down again, driving you to crave more of the foods that will increase your glucose levels quickly and give you a short-lasting energy fix.

We want to avoid extremes when it comes to emotional eating and bingeing. If your glucose levels fluctuate moderately, you'll be far less prone to experiencing physical cravings or other symptoms typically associated with the need to use food as a coping mechanism.

Please refer back to the *Balanced Plate* outlined in chapter 8. These guidelines are designed to help you maintain stable glucose levels without resorting to obsessive weighing and measuring of food. It's also important to recognise that stabilising glucose is not the only consideration when it comes to deciding what to put on your plate.

18. ENDING FOOD CHAOS

Typical eating patterns like skipping breakfast, continuous snacking, daytime starvation followed by night-time eating, and the consumption of nutritionally deficient foods, as well as engaging in bingeing and restricting, all contribute to various chemical imbalances within the body which we'll look at shortly.

In order for your body to be able to manufacture the substances you need to maintain chemical balance, you must supply the raw materials they are made of. These consist of complex carbohydrates, adequate fat and protein, vitamins, minerals, and phytonutrients (natural compounds found in plant foods).

A varied and diverse diet will assist with the steady release of brain chemicals known as neurotransmitters. These help to promote positive feelings, healthy sleep patterns, reduce the risk of impulsive behaviour, and restore your appetite system.

THE LOOP OF CHAOS

EATING BEHAVIOURS
dietary chaos, restriction, binging

FOOD IMBALANCE
high caffeine, high artificial sweeteners, low fibre, low protein, imbalance of fats, lack of diversity

NUTRIENT DEFICIENCIES
destabilised blood glucose, low vitamins, minerals, amino acids, fibre, essential fats

EFFECT ON BODY
brain chemical imbalance, poor digestive function, hormone imbalance, slower metabolism, sleep problems,

UNPLEASANT SYMPTOMS
high hunger, high stress, high anxiety, weight gain, low mood, low energy

A Note on What Happens to Food When We Eat

The process of eating is far more complex than the popular notion that we eat, then move to burn those calories, finally pooping out what is left. It can be helpful to understand the basics of what actually occurs in your digestive system when you eat:

- The process starts when you see and smell your food which helps trigger the release of digestive enzymes in your saliva
- Tasting and chewing your food, with the help of digestive enzymes, begins to digest carbohydrates in your mouth
- Various digestive enzymes within your digestive tract, in addition to stomach acid, facilitate the breakdown of your food into absorbable nutrients
- The microbes in your gut feed on the food you eat to produce essential chemicals and nutrients
- The nutrients are absorbed through your gut wall into the bloodstream to be used throughout your body
- You eliminate waste products via the body's detoxification systems, involving processes such as bowel movements, urination, and sweating

Food Chaos and Brain Chemicals

Serotonin is a potent mood-enhancing neurotransmitter, released after eating carbohydrates or sugar[78]. Notably, insufficient levels of serotonin can trigger cravings[79]. Furthermore, prolonged episodes of bingeing or compulsive eating of sugary or refined carbohydrate foods may downregulate your serotonin receptors over time, potentially intensifying urges and cravings for these foods[80].

THE BINGE FREEDOM METHOD

TIP: The essential amino acid tryptophan (among other nutrients) is necessary to produce this vital brain chemical. Tryptophan can be found in dairy, meat, bananas, beans, fish, lentils, oats, poultry, and seeds[81]. For more details on food sources of nutrients, please refer to the table in the additional resource section at the back of the book.

GABA (gamma-aminobutyric acid) is a neurotransmitter that often plays a role in eating behaviour. Known for reducing stress, relieving anxiety, and promoting relaxation, it may help stabilise appetite, prevent extreme blood glucose dips, and reduce stress-driven eating.

TIP: GABA is produced in the brain from the amino acid glutamate with the help of vitamin B6. Foods like tomatoes, mushrooms, dairy, eggs, fish, meat and seafood support this process. Theanine, an amino acid found in green and black tea, also aids GABA, serotonin, and dopamine production and is available as an L-theanine supplement. For more on food sources, see the table in the additional resources section at the back of the book.

Acetylcholine is a neurotransmitter involved in motivation, memory, digestion and appetite. It also plays a key role in the brain's reward system by regulating dopamine. Choline and vitamin B5 are essential for making this brain chemical, so including foods rich in these nutrients is important.

TIP: Choline and vitamin B5 are found in many of the same foods, including eggs, tofu, fish, mushrooms, organ meats and whole grains. For more on food sources, see the table in the additional resources section at the back of the book.

Endorphins serve as natural pain relievers that also influence your mood. These are produced by the body during pleasurable activity such as eating. They promote the release of the neurotransmitter dopamine which is responsible for reward and pleasure[82].

Research has shown that chaotic eating habits can disrupt the reward circuits of the brain[83]. Consequently, the brain may become less responsive to the rewarding effects of dopamine, potentially leading to increased compulsive eating as an attempt to seek pleasure.

The good news is that restoring balance and consistency to your eating patterns can help to address this issue[84]. For a reminder on maintaining regular mealtimes, please revisit chapter 3.

> **TIP:** Dopamine relies on the amino acid phenylalanine for its production. Sources include animal proteins, beans, lentils, nuts, seeds, wholegrains and tofu.

As the examples above indicate, a diverse and balanced diet will provide the essential nutrients your body needs to support the production of neurotransmitters, which are vital for regulating your mood, motivation, cravings, and hunger.

> **A Note on Reward Deficiency Syndrome**
> There is an uncommon condition known as Reward Deficiency Syndrome. Individuals with this condition have been found to have fewer dopamine receptors in their brain increasing the likelihood of binge-type behaviours and weight gain.

☆ Client Story

Alice

Dramatic Improvement in Eating Habits, Mood, Energy, and Sleep

I met Alice whilst she was studying at university. When she first came to me for help, her eating was extremely chaotic, and she was desperate to overcome binge eating. Alice frequently skipped breakfast, occasionally grabbing a sandwich, and relied on diet soda drinks throughout the day. Upon returning home, she would continue to snack throughout the evening. Alongside these eating challenges, she struggled with low mood, diminished motivation, poor sleep, and fatigue, often finding it difficult to muster the energy to attend her classes.

Alice recognised that she paid little attention to what she ate and was prepared to start introducing one meal at a time. She began with her evening meal, opting for something really simple that she could quickly assemble with minimal effort. At first, she would prepare a meal using ready-cooked chicken, a packet of mixed ready-to-heat whole grains, and a salad bag and then slowly introduced more options. Next, she began to swap out her diet drinks. By preparing a large bottle of water with fresh mint leaves to carry with her, Alice was able to reduce her daily diet drink intake from three or four to just one.

Throughout her journey, Alice noticed a positive shift in her mood and increased motivation, empowering her to explore more diverse meal ideas.

She incorporated breakfast into her routine, discovering two or three options that she genuinely enjoyed. Alice was now sleeping undisturbed through the night and her cravings had markedly decreased. She no longer felt compelled to snack on crisps, pastries, and chocolate. She was amazed at her own progress, exclaiming 'I can't believe I am finally free of this,' during one of her sessions.

Have You Switched from Sugar to Artificial Sweeteners?

There is a common misconception that swapping sugar for artificial sweeteners is the solution to removing sugar from your diet. While too much sugar is unhelpful, substances like sucralose (found in products like Splenda and Canderel) and aspartame (a key ingredient in Diet Coke) have been shown to negatively affect blood glucose levels and the balance of bacteria in your gut[85] [86] [87] [88].

A 2021 study[89] – one of the largest to date – has examined how the brain responds to sucralose. It found that the sweetener increases activity in regions of the brain responsible for food cravings and appetite, affecting both women and individuals classified as clinically overweight. Additionally, there was an observed decrease in the body's satiety hormones that tell you when you are full. Not quite so helpful for those wanting to take control of bingeing, emotional eating, and snacking after all.

TIP: Natural sweeteners, such as pure maple syrup or pure stevia, are better options as sugar alternatives. By gradually reducing the sweetness of your food, you will find that your taste buds require less of it.

Do You Always Choose Low-Fat Options?

Low-fat foods can contribute to dietary chaos in several ways. Frequently, the fat content is substituted with sugar, artificial sweeteners, and additives in these products. This can lead to an insufficient intake of essential natural fats necessary for hormone production and brain function, often leaving you feeling unsatisfied after a meal[90]. (Refer back to chapter 6 for further insights into the significance of fats in your diet.)

19. ADDING IN (NOT STRIPPING OUT)

It's estimated that one in three people are deficient in at least ten minerals. This is partly because the food we eat now is around 30% less nutritious than the same food in the 1940s, due to modern farming methods and eroded soils[91]. Consequently, when disordered eating is part of the picture, it contributes to a perfect storm affecting our physiological function and our capacity to cope.

If a significant portion of your calorie intake is derived from binge trigger foods and your eating is inconsistent and chaotic, it's probable that your diet is lacking diversity. Transitioning to a varied diet will provide an array of nutrients required for the optimal functioning of biological processes within the body. These nutrients are essentially the raw materials necessary for the production of energy, hormones, and brain chemicals.

What About Supplements?
You cannot supplement your way out of a chaotic diet. Food must come first. Supplements can be helpful to plug gaps, but in general, recommendations need to be tailored to the individual.

I have outlined some key supplements here, but it's advisable to seek guidance from a qualified nutrition professional. They can provide individualised advice, considering factors such as dosage, the best nutrient form, and check for potential interactions with medications.

Supplement	Why Needed	Considerations
Vitamin D	Mostly obtained from sunlight exposure. Required by those living in northern latitudes	The dose will depend on a variety of factors. Blood testing is recommended to determine a suitable dose.
DHA and EPA omega-3 (Available in fish oil or vegan algae form)	May be required if your diet excludes oily fish such as salmon, mackerel, herring, anchovies, sardines	Consult your doctor first, if you are taking medication.
Vitamin B12	May be required if your diet excludes or is limited in fish, poultry, meat, eggs, and dairy	Ideally test blood serum levels before supplementing.
Iron	May be required if your diet excludes or is limited in fish, poultry, meat, eggs, and dairy	Serum iron levels must be tested before supplementing.
Zinc	May be required if your diet excludes or is limited in fish, poultry, meat, eggs, and dairy	Ideally take this at night before bed unless you are taking zinc as part of a multivitamin and mineral supplement.
Digestive enzymes	This can be helpful if you suffer with bloating which is often a symptom of binge eating. More on this in chapter 22	Take with each meal.

The nutrient table in the additional resource section at the back of the book illustrates the influence of micronutrients when incorporated into your diet. By including these nutrients via the food you eat, you will not only enhance your energy levels, mood[92], and stress-coping abilities but also naturally displace the less beneficial foods. Consequently, this can significantly impact your eating behaviour.

20. HAPPY HORMONES?

Hormones play a greater role in our eating habits than you might think. Whether directly regulating appetite or contributing to other functions, we cannot underestimate the interconnected nature of our biology[93] [94].

The following insights will shed light on the intricate relationship between your eating habits and lifestyle and its influence on crucial hormones, as well as how these hormones reciprocally impact your eating behaviours!

The Hunger Hormone Ghrelin

The hunger hormone ghrelin is released when your stomach empties. It activates hunger, feeding, and food-seeking areas of your brain.

It's important to note that lack of good-quality sleep leads to more ghrelin production, essentially increasing your appetite and, incidentally, this slows the fat-burning process[95]. An interesting study found that participants' appetite for high-carb foods increased by 32% after two days of severely curtailed sleep[96].

The Satiety Hormone Leptin

Leptin does the opposite job of ghrelin by telling us when we are full. This is also negatively affected by poor sleep, contributing to an increased appetite and slower metabolism[97]. We will examine the role of sleep in more detail in chapter 24.

The Stress Hormone Cortisol

The stress hormone cortisol, that helps you to respond to immediate danger, needs a mention too. It impacts your physiology by increasing your heart rate, blood pressure, and blood glucose availability, providing energy for your muscles for a 'fight or flight' scenario[98].

Issues arise with prolonged activation of cortisol, which happens when you consistently experience stress. Too much cortisol in the body can trigger a cascade of problems leading to afternoon crashes, fatigue, anxiety, and sugar cravings[99] [100]. Chronic stress also reduces your sensitivity to insulin and hampers your body's effectiveness in processing blood glucose. Strategies for managing stress to give you alternative coping mechanisms will be explored later in chapter 40.

The Blood Sugar Hormone Insulin

We covered insulin's role in regulating your blood glucose in chapter 17, but did you know that it is also involved in regulating your appetite? After eating, your brain will sense there is more insulin in the body and send messages so that you feel less hunger. Some studies suggest that insulin resistance (where your body's cells have become less responsive to insulin due to prolonged exposure to high levels of glucose) may hinder its ability to perform this task of suppressing your hunger[101].

The Satiety Hormone GLP-1

GLP-1 is released when we digest food. It slows down how quickly our stomach empties, helps release insulin, and makes us feel full[102]. You might have heard of GLP-1 because of semaglutide, a weight loss injection popularised by Hollywood celebrities. Semaglutide mimics the effects of GLP-1 in the body and is also used, in lower doses, to treat diabetes.

However, these injections have drawbacks, especially when given at the higher dose intended for weight loss. Common side effects include nausea, vomiting, and other gastrointestinal issues. This medication also carries an increased risk of developing a serious disease, including pancreatitis, gallbladder disease, and even thyroid cancer[103]. Furthermore, when you discontinue the medication, you are likely to regain any weight lost[104].

The Fullness Hormone CCK

CCK (cholecystokinin) is a potent appetite hormone that tells you when you are full during a meal (as opposed to between meals) and supports the digestive process. It is released when food stretches stomach receptors and enters the small intestine. CCK travels from your gallbladder to the gut, into the bloodstream and eventually reaches your brain. Increased CCK levels in the blood can be detected 15 minutes after your meal has begun and levels remain raised for the next three hours[105]. This emphasises the significance of slowing down while eating, giving your brain the chance to catch up with your stomach and signal that you are full. Mindful eating can help with this process and is a topic we'll delve into shortly.

HOW YOUR APPETITE WORKS

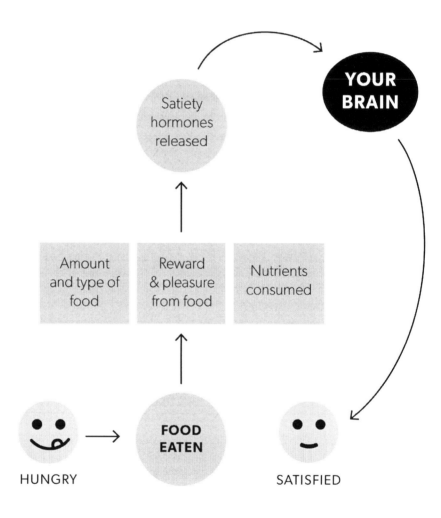

Adapted from Blundell JE, Rogers PJ, Hill AJ.

The Hunger Brain Chemical NPY
NPY (neuropeptide Y), along with serotonin and dopamine, plays a direct role in triggering cravings. NPY is released in the brain region that responds to our emotional experiences and memories[106]. This provides a connection between eating and mood. It is common for emotional eaters to mistake emotional cues (such as stress, boredom, or sadness) for hunger. We will look at this in greater depth in chapter 33.

As you work towards achieving balance in your eating habits, the less helpful foods will naturally make up a smaller proportion of your diet. By making other foods interesting and tasty, you can increase their appeal, bring satisfaction to your overall eating experience, and reduce cravings for binge foods.

Your Menstrual Cycle
The two all-important female sex hormones, oestrogen and progesterone should also be acknowledged. Oestrogen is one of the key reproductive hormones, but did you know that it also reduces appetite? Furthermore, when oestrogen levels drop prior to menstruation, it takes the brain chemicals dopamine and serotonin down with it, in some cases leading to extreme sugar cravings and increased appetite before your period starts.

The hormone progesterone, known for playing a key role in the menstrual cycle, has a stimulating effect on appetite and high levels can raise insulin. Around 14 days prior to menstruation, when progesterone peaks and oestrogen is relatively low, heightened insulin may also contribute to increased sugar cravings and hunger.

Throughout your reproductive years, progesterone should be present to counterbalance oestrogen's natural cyclical fluctuations. Sufficient progesterone production has a calming effect on the brain and helps you to cope with stress[107].

Perimenopause

The menopause transition is a pivotal time when challenges around food and body image can emerge, resurface, or worsen[108] [109]. If you are approaching this life stage, you might have already observed changes in your eating behaviours. Binge and emotional eating often develop as a coping mechanism when life feels overwhelming and out of control.

Roller-coastering oestrogen levels, that eventually fall, alongside declining progesterone levels often lead to symptoms including anxiety, depression, sleep disturbances, and cognitive decline. Moreover, the extreme rise and fall in oestrogen levels experienced during perimenopause can also bring about intense cravings[110].

Simultaneously, many women juggle the responsibilities of caring for elderly parents and adjusting to grown children leaving home. For some, this phase coincides with the breakdown of their marriage, adding to feelings of loss and overwhelm.

Changes in body shape and weight are common as women navigate perimenopause. New oestrogen lows, coupled with declining progesterone, can cause metabolic changes that lead to weight gain around the middle. During this time, women experience a 15% drop in metabolic rate (calories burned at rest) due to reduced muscle retention and a shift towards insulin resistance. This is a major factor in abdominal weight gain, and women with a history of PCOS (polycystic ovary syndrome) are at higher risk of developing menopausal insulin resistance and weight gain.

Additionally, while thyroid disease develops independently of perimenopause, this life phase can exacerbate autoimmune conditions like Hashimoto's due to immune system recalibration. This affects the production of thyroid hormones which play a crucial role in regulating metabolism.

Many women find it distressing that their previous eating and exercise routines no longer work for them, often leading to extreme dieting behaviour, followed by compulsive eating. Some women feel such as sense of hopelessness that turning to food becomes their only option.

A complex system of communication exists among all hormones, where some suppress and some trigger the release of hormones. If you struggle with poor sleep, high stress, anxiety, digestive problems, or poor blood glucose control, the intricate feedback mechanisms may not be working at their best. Further insights on how to help address these issues will be explored in later chapters.

For those experiencing the menopause, this is a time when associated symptoms can exacerbate those of attention deficit hyperactivity disorder (ADHD)[111]. It's not uncommon for women in midlife to only recognise that they have ADHD when going through the perimenopause. To understand why this is relevant, let's now look at the relationship between ADHD and binge eating[112].

21. ADHD AND BINGE EATING

Approximately, 30% of binge eaters are thought to also have ADHD[113]. The association is believed to be due to several factors. The impulsivity seen in people with ADHD is believed to play a role, as it affects executive functions such as planning and organisation[114]. Some people with ADHD become hyperfocused on tasks, sometimes forgetting to eat at regular mealtimes, often leading to extreme hunger and cravings later in the day[115]. This commonly results in nutritional deficiencies that contribute to ADHD symptoms, and so the cycle continues.

People with ADHD have been found to have lower levels of available dopamine, with the brain being less effective at receiving it[116]. As mentioned earlier, dopamine is linked to feelings of reward and pleasure, as well as motivation and focus. Eating something tasty will stimulate the release of dopamine, creating a sense of pleasure. Carbohydrate-rich foods can contribute to this positive feeling by providing an immediate boost of dopamine. While there is nothing wrong with using food as a source of stimulation, combining it with some protein will enhance your satisfaction and keep your blood glucose stable.

You may be constantly seeking more pleasure from food if you are not getting enough dopamine. This lack of dopamine may also be impacting your ability to organise yourself and plan.

If you are struggling with the symptoms of ADHD, please revisit chapter 12. The planning techniques will be especially important to help support you to eat balanced meals regularly.

☆ **Client Story**

Julie

Overcoming Binge Eating with the Challenges of ADHD

I met Julie when she was 33, shortly after she had received her ADHD diagnosis. Throughout her life, she had struggled with an unhealthy relationship with food and uncontrollable compulsions to eat. Managing simple tasks involving organisation and self-care proved challenging for Julie. Working from home, she would become hyperfocused on her work tasks, often forgetting to eat, leading to intense cravings and bingeing later in the day. This was compounded by Julie's inability to identify her hunger until it overwhelmed her with extreme intensity. Furthermore, her daily eating lacked any planning which contributed to an overall sense of chaos in her life.

Julie worked on a simple plan to ensure she had something prepared for lunch. Her partner tended to cook a balanced meal in the evening (which she often skipped due to grazing or bingeing late in the afternoon), so she asked that he cook double portions in order to have leftovers for the next day's lunch. Julie then began to eat food with her partner in the evening. She managed lunchtimes by setting an alarm to stop and eat, even if she didn't feel particularly hungry. These adjustments helped to not only improve her mood but also reduced her overwhelming cravings.

Julie progressed to planning her breakfasts and worked out timings to make this possible. Instead of spending an extra half hour in bed scrolling on her phone in the morning, she began to get up and prepare a simple breakfast of porridge, fruit, and seeds. We approached this process with caution, ensuring not to introduce too many changes simultaneously to prevent overwhelm. She found this approach manageable, which gave her the confidence and motivation to believe that she could conquer her challenges and regain a sense of control.

22. THE GUT CONNECTION

Have you ever considered that issues with your hunger signals may be linked to the health of your gut?

Your digestive system is home to billions of bacteria and other microbes, now recognised as an organ in its own right, called the microbiome. The microbes are a balance of beneficial bacteria, opportunistic microbes, and potentially harmful bacteria. Your gut microbiome functions like a biological factory where the microbes maintain an intricate bidirectional relationship with your body's cells. It lies within your digestive system, which is the tube that runs from your mouth to your anus.

A diverse microbiome, with a balance of many species of helpful bacteria, is essential for supporting your metabolism and maintaining healthy glucose levels. The microbes in your gut influence how your body stores and uses energy, particularly by extracting energy from undigested, resistant starch and fibre within the digestive tract.[117]

Additionally, your microbiome plays a key role in producing various brain chemicals including dopamine and serotonin, while also helping to regulate appetite[118].

An imbalance in the microbiome has the potential to disrupt satiety, affecting hormones that signal fullness, and may even play a role in thyroid problems which can affect your metabolism[119]. We will explore approaches to support your microbiome later in this chapter.

A Vicious Cycle

It's extremely common for individuals who struggle with their eating to suffer with co-occurring digestive issues such as bloating, constipation, diarrhoea, and acid reflux. These symptoms are frequently reported by those who struggle with binge eating[120]. About 44% of people with irritable bowel syndrome (IBS)-type symptoms (which include bloating, constipation, diarrhoea, and gas) are disordered eaters, and 98% of people with eating disorders have co-occurring gut problems[121]. It is no coincidence, as digestive symptoms correlate with psychological distress. Furthermore, eating behaviours that disrupt digestion, lead to changes in the physiology of the gut and an imbalance in the microbiome.

This often results in a recurring pattern – gut discomfort and pain leading to further food restriction in order to manage symptoms. Digestive complaints may also lead to the desire to eliminate certain foods, even when your diet does not relieve symptoms.

Even if you do not experience digestive symptoms, your unwanted eating patterns are likely to influence the health of your gut. This sets up a challenging cycle where binge or emotional eating affect the digestive system, influencing your brain chemicals, metabolism, and appetite, and in turn, maintaining emotional and binge eating behaviours.[122]

Is bloating a trigger for you?

If bloating is something you experience and it impacts how you feel about your body, it's helpful to understand what might be going on and know that you can improve your digestive function. **Important Note: if you encounter persistent bloating, it's important to seek guidance from your doctor to rule out a serious underlying cause.**

A Note on Digestive Enzymes

These are released by the pancreas and in the small intestine to break down food into its individual nutrients in order to be absorbed through the gut wall and into the bloodstream. If this enzyme system works ineffectively, undigested food will be fermented by gut bacteria causing gas, bloating, and irregular bowel movements. Your digestive function may be improved by using digestive enzyme supplements. These must be taken with meals, just as you begin to eat.

Other factors

Chaotic eating patterns and timing, such as on-the-go eating, frequent snacking, or skipping meals are likely to affect the gut lining which can impact overall digestive health. Various other factors may play a role too, these include:

- Processed foods – including additives, colours, emulsifiers, flavours, preservatives, and sweeteners
- Effects of medications and medical procedures
- Restrictive diets, and changing from one diet to the next

Note: Eating a low-fat diet can negatively impact your digestive system. This is because good-quality fats are needed to make bile[123], a powerful substance that helps you to detoxify waste products and keep your gallbladder healthy for better digestion.

How to Help Your Gut Help You

It is early days in terms of research, but what we do know is that by nurturing your gut you will improve your well-being across the board. By being mindful of what, when, and how you eat, you can actively contribute to supporting your gut and, in turn, help to manage your eating behaviour.

❖ **What** – diet diversity

Eating a wide variety of colourful plant foods throughout the week will help support the diversity of your microbiome[124] [125], as each microbe thrives on its own preferred food. This practice also helps your microbes to produce special gut-supporting substances called short-chain fatty acids (SCFA)[126]. Incorporate all types of vegetables, whole grains, nuts, seeds, and lentils and beans (if tolerated). Try to include foods that will specifically increase your SCFA levels, such as stewed apple, oats, and flaxseeds.

You can also try fermented foods if you enjoy them; these can be beneficial for improving the bacterial diversity in your gut (examples include miso, sauerkraut, kimchi, kefir, tempeh, natto, and kombucha). Try to steer clear of foods containing artificial sweeteners.

Note: Yoghurt is produced by bacterial fermentation of milk, yet commercially made yoghurts typically lose their live cultures due to the pasteurisation process. Go for organic varieties, if possible, which are more likely to contain probiotic cultures.

What About Probiotics?
We are learning increasingly about the benefit of taking a probiotic supplement. It is no longer thought that probiotics help by replacing missing bacteria but more that they help to create the best environment for beneficial bacteria to grow. (A good analogy is how to think about creating the best conditions in your garden for plants and insects to thrive.) It is best to consult a qualified nutrition practitioner to get advice on a product with specific probiotic strains to suit your needs.

⚡ Action Step

INCREASE THE VARIETY OF PLANT FOODS IN YOUR DIET TO SUPPORT YOUR GUT MICROBIOME AND HELP REGULATE YOUR APPETITE HORMONES

Think about what new foods you can add to your diet to help your microbiome flourish. Use the 30 plants a week resource below (which you can also download at www.marcellerosenutrition/book-resources).

Start to build up slowly – begin by counting the number of different plant foods you eat in a week and aim to add an additional 5 in the following week and so on until you eventually reach 30. Keep in mind that diverse plant foods include the various colours and varieties of the same plant, as well as herbs and spices. Note down every food only once within the next 7 days to assess your diet diversity.

30 Plants in a week					

❖ **When** – breakfast, lunch, and dinner. Try to have a gap between meals and avoid continuous grazing. (Refer back to chapter 3.)

❖ **How** – master how to eat mindfully (we will cover this shortly in chapter 26).

23. YOUR VAGUS SUPERHIGHWAY

When you feel anxious, stressed, or wired, the sympathetic branch of your nervous system initiates the fight or flight response in your body. This may occur when you find yourself overthinking or catastrophising, especially if you think you have breached one of your diet rules. While this stress response is important for survival, it's harmful to consistently be in this state.

It is possible to encourage a shift to the parasympathetic nervous system, also known as the rest and digest state, which relaxes the body after episodes of stress. You can encourage this by stimulating your vagus nerve[127] (see below). This nerve extends from your brain down to your stomach, carrying signals to your organs and transmitting messages back to your brain. When your vagus nerve is activated, it can send a signal to slow your heart rate and lower your blood pressure telling your body to calm down[128] [129].

Transitioning into the rest and digest state offers various advantages:

- It helps to improve digestion, allowing the body to absorb nutrients more effectively and reduce digestive symptoms[130]
- It assists in balancing mood and the ability to cope with difficult feelings[131]
- It helps to build a more resilient nervous system, supporting recovery from anxiety and stress[132]

⚡ **Action Step**

DAILY PRACTICE TO STIMULATE YOUR VAGUS NERVE

Choose one of the activities below to encourage the activation of your vagus nerve[133]:

- Exposure to cold water – this may involve splashing cold water on your face and hands, applying a cold compress to your neck or chest, or taking a cold shower (though the latter may not always be practical in the moment!)[134 135 136].

- Humming – consider doing this before facing a situation that triggers anxiety[137].

- Singing loudly – try belting out a tune whenever you have the opportunity, such as in the shower or car[138].

- Gargling – this is a way of contracting the muscles at the back of the throat which also activates the vagus nerve. Every morning, take a glass of water, gargle one sip at a time, and then swallow until you finish the glass.

- Deep, slow breathing from your belly. (This is covered in greater detail in chapter 40.)[139]

Think about when one of these techniques can be introduced into your daily routine.

24. RHYTHMIC RESET

The Master Clock

Your daily circadian rhythm consists of natural cycles in the body that occur approximately every 24 hours. They are controlled by a master body clock which directs every aspect of your metabolism[140] and causes physiological change throughout your body, rather like the conductor of an orchestra. These rhythms influence the release of insulin[141], cortisol, and the important sleep hormone, melatonin in addition to detoxification, hunger, digestion, and the uptake of fats. So, it's no surprise that there is a known correlation between binge eating and circadian rhythm disruption[142].

What Disrupts Your Circadian Rhythm?

Your natural body clock can become impaired through artificial light[143], chronic stress, shift work[144] and jet lag[145]. Using screens and bright lighting late at night coupled with limited exposure to daylight, particularly in the early part of the day, may affect not only your sleep-wake cycle but also other internal rhythms. Frequent eating, night eating, restrictive eating, and bingeing can also play a role, as meal timing serves as one of the external signals influencing the central master clock[146 147]. This underscores the importance of maintaining regular meal patterns.

In the previous chapter, we explored the gut microbiome and its potential influence on your appetite. Notably, we are learning more about how bacteria in your gut may impact your circadian rhythm. So, there will be additional benefits if you are already working on increasing the diversity of your food.

Appetite and Cravings

It may come as a surprise to learn that eating late increases hunger and reduces the satiety hormone leptin[148], so you are less likely to feel satisfied and may also have an increased desire to eat later in the day. In addition to increasing hunger and food intake, disrupted rhythms will also affect your food choices, with an increased propensity to choose refined carbohydrates and sugary foods. Late eating also reduces the amount of energy you burn when awake and seems to favour fat storage[149].

Remember if you are trying to 'save' calories by postponing when you eat your first meal of the day, you are far more likely to consume more later on. Furthermore, your metabolism will operate most efficiently when your body receives its meals in accordance with its internal clock, allowing it to anticipate regular eating times[150]. Eating late at night, when your body is not ready for food, is likely to compromise your metabolism and disrupt the balance of leptin and ghrelin.

If you are still having 'diet mindset thoughts' and worrying about your weight – let me remind you that the body is complex and that there are many variables that influence your weight. Disrupted circadian rhythm and inadequate sleep have been identified to play a significant role in weight gain. Moreover, there is evidence suggesting that these factors speed up the loss of lean body mass and impair fat loss, influencing overall body composition[151].

How to Support a Healthy Circadian Rhythm

Quality sleep (and enough of it) is essential for key body processes needed for a well-balanced circadian rhythm. Even if you don't think your sleep is much of a problem, it's a good idea to establish a healthy sleep pattern.

How Sleep Affects Eating

Sleep and eating are two essential components of self-care, and they are closely interconnected. The quality and quantity of your sleep can affect your appetite and food choices[152], while the food you eat can impact the quality of your sleep[153].

Ideally, as an adult, you need between seven and nine hours of good-quality sleep a night. Sleep deprivation has been found to cause extreme swings of emotional highs and lows[154], in addition to cravings and addictions. Inadequate sleep increases appetite and the desire to snack[155]. It prevents weight loss when actively trying to lose weight due to higher levels of the stress hormone cortisol. It may be that you are fixated on a healthy diet and exercise regime but disregarding the necessity for quality sleep.

Sleep is vital for regulating the hormones that control hunger and satiety[156]. When you don't get enough, your body produces more ghrelin, the hormone that stimulates hunger, and less leptin, the hormone that signals when you are full. This hormonal imbalance can lead to overeating and cravings for the less helpful foods.

In addition to affecting appetite hormones, lack of sleep can also affect the prefrontal cortex, the part of the brain responsible for decision-making and impulse control[157]. The lower brain is responsible for primal instincts and the habitual drive to seek pleasure and avoid pain. When you're tired, you're more likely to make impulsive food choices and go for options providing immediate but short-lived pleasure and energy.

In light of this, let's explore what steps you can take to improve the quality of your sleep and to help to maintain a balanced circadian rhythm.

How Eating Affects Sleep

What you eat and when you eat can also affect your sleep. Certain foods, such as those high in sugar and caffeine, can disrupt sleep patterns and make it harder to fall asleep[158].

Eating a heavy meal close to bedtime can make it more difficult to fall asleep because your body is still digesting the food. Instead, aim to eat your last meal at least two to three hours before bedtime. It's also important to eat enough during the day and balance your meals with protein, natural fats, a variety of vegetables, and slow-releasing carbohydrates to help regulate your blood glucose. A diet high in starchy carbohydrates such as bread, rice, pasta, and sugars will increase your insulin production. This can lead to fluctuations in night-time blood glucose levels, which may cause sleep disruptions.

Nutrients and Foods that May Help with Your Sleep:
Magnesium is an important mineral required for relaxation of our muscles and mind. It also improves melatonin and cortisol production. It can be found in green, leafy vegetables, nuts, seeds, and beans. This mineral can be topped up with a supplement – opt for magnesium bisglycinate or glycinate which is the best absorbed and the most effective form for sleep[159 160].

Vitamin D has been found to reduce the time it takes to fall asleep and to improve sleep. Low levels have been associated with sleep apnoea, restless leg syndrome and short sleep duration[161]. Vitamin D deficiency is very common in the northern hemisphere, so it's worth having a blood test to check your levels.

Tryptophan is an *essential* amino acid, meaning that we must obtain it from our diet[162]. It is required to make serotonin, and serotonin is needed to make the 'sleep hormone' melatonin[163]. Tryptophan can be found in dairy products, eggs, red meat, poultry, fish, oats, dried dates, chickpeas, almonds, sunflower and pumpkin seeds, bananas, and peanuts. Complex carbohydrates help tryptophan to get past the blood-brain barrier to reach the brain, hence a snack containing protein *and* complex carbs is recommended in the evening.

Light and Dark

Our brain takes clues from light and darkness. The release of the sleep-inducing hormone melatonin starts at dusk. Conversely, the stress hormone cortisol is triggered by morning light. Due to the use of artificial light, our modern life no longer provides these cues which disrupts this delicate hormone balance.

The following can help to keep this in check:

- Set a regular time each morning to go outside for at least 30 minutes (within 1-2 hrs of waking) to reset your circadian clock.

- Make your bedroom pitch black for sleep – use blackout blinds, an eye mask, and ensure there are no electrical lights/LEDs in your room and dim the lights at least an hour before bed.

By paying attention to your sleep and making small changes where necessary, you can improve your chances of making more helpful food choices the next day. Approach this with self-compassion and without becoming overly fixated, as worrying will lead to stress, which (you guessed it) will impact your sleep and eating behaviours!

Are You a Shift Worker?

If you work shifts, this can have a significant impact on your appetite, cravings and eating behaviour[164]. You are more likely to crave refined carbohydrates and sugary foods and will be less efficient at processing your food[165].

I recommend eating a balanced meal just before your shift that contains protein, natural fats, and fibre-rich food for that slow energy release. Then eat a balanced meal for breakfast before your daytime sleep.

Try to avoid eating between midnight and 6 a.m. if possible, but if you need a snack in the night ensure you have something protein and fibre-rich.

Snack ideas include hard-boiled eggs, fruit, unsalted nuts, hummus and pre-cut vegetables, or oatcakes (also refer to the list in chapter 13 for ideas).

Ensure you continue to drink water throughout your night shift and avoid caffeinated drinks.

Are You a Frequent Flyer?

Try the following if you frequently cross time zones and regularly experience jet lag:

- Avoid alcohol and caffeine during the flight but stay hydrated with plenty of water
- Switch to your new bedtime as soon as possible and avoid long naps during the day
- Expose yourself to early morning sun/daylight in your new destination

Could Bright Light Therapy help?

Studies show that bright light therapy is effective for treating seasonal and non-seasonal depression[166]. Additionally, research indicates that exposure to morning bright light can reduce binge eating and food preoccupation[167] [168].

Bright light therapy can help you 'reset' your circadian clock if used early in the day[169]. LED day lights can be purchased in the form of light boxes, lamps, and alarm clocks. With an output of 10,000 lux bright, full spectrum light, you would only need 15 to 30 minutes of exposure per day.

For shift work: Try bright light therapy in the evening if you regularly work during the night. In this case, it's important to avoid daylight as much as possible when you finish work and go to bed. Dark sunglasses or special blue light-blocking glasses may help.

For jet lag: Try bright light therapy in the morning when travelling east and in the evening when travelling west.

☆ **Client Story**

Beth

Shift Work, Poor Sleep, and Binge Eating

Beth worked as a junior doctor on a busy ward that involved various day and night shifts. She was a chronic yo-yo dieter, describing herself as repeatedly falling on and off the wagon with the potential for day-long binge episodes.

Beth's sleep quality was consistently poor, she often took a long time to fall asleep. During nights off, she would spend prolonged hours awake on her phone and, after night shifts, she tended to stay in bed all day which left her feeling down. The hospital where Beth worked was close to a convenience store, and Beth would often pick up snacks that made her cravings worse. Moreover, the stress levels she experienced at work were considerable, and eating became a source of solace, sustaining her through the night.

We explored finding the best mealtimes to accommodate her various shifts. Incorporating breakfast proved transformative, establishing consistency in her eating. Beth invested in a daylight lamp and a new alarm clock, keeping her phone outside her bedroom and began reading instead of scrolling before going to sleep.

These combined strategies led to better sleep, a significant reduction in binge episodes, and an improved mood. Beth acknowledged this as a pivotal milestone on her journey, providing the encouragement needed to continue progressing.

⚡ Action Step

Devise your personalised sleep plan below to help reset your circadian rhythm, improve your motivation and energy, and keep your appetite hormones in check.

Use the table below to implement the following strategies over time into your daily routine. To prevent overwhelm, avoid trying to introduce all of these at once.

Sleep Plan Strategy	Actioned	Notes
Avoid caffeine later in the day and limit alcohol before bedtime. Both can interfere with sleep patterns and cause you to wake up during the night[170] [171]. (Refer back to chapter 14 for more on this)		
Try some gentle movement or activity during the day to improve restful sleep. A brisk morning walk ticks this box with the added benefit of light exposure during the day (more on movement in chapter 41)		

Sleep Plan Strategy	Actioned	Notes
Continue to regulate your blood sugar with regular balanced meals and eat enough during the day! You also want to avoid going to bed physically hungry. If needed, have a snack before bed – a glass of milk or banana with a few almonds are ideal. If you wake up in the middle of the night, it could be due to a drop in blood sugar		
Stick to a consistent sleep schedule. Try to go to bed and wake up at the same time every day, even on weekends, and avoid napping during the day		
Create a relaxing bedtime routine. Take a warm bath, read a book, or listen to calming music before bedtime to help your body and mind relax		
Try to make your bedroom dark at night (with blackout binds or use an eye mask) and a little bit cool		
Clear your mind – keep a bedside journal to jot things down that may worry you		

Sleep Plan Strategy	Actioned	Notes
Before bed, avoid stimulating activities such as watching an edge-of-the-seat film or having an important conversation		
Avoid using your phone or tablet before bed as they emit the same blue light as the morning sun. If you need to use your phone, you may be able to set it to amber light display after dark or try blue light-blocking glasses. Avoid engaging with social media which is also stimulating and negatively impacts sleep[172]		
Switch to a traditional alarm clock so your smartphone can stay out of the bedroom		
Eating plan for shift work Refer to the section 'Are You a Shift Worker?'		
Jet lag plan Refer to the section 'Are You a Frequent Flyer?' above		

25. UNDERSTANDING YOUR APPETITE

One of the questions I'm most frequently asked is, 'How do I know when I'm really hungry or not?' Many people find it challenging to recognise when they feel full or satisfied and may unintentionally eat to the point of extreme discomfort. Being uncomfortably full commonly triggers feelings of shame and regret after a binge eating episode and can exacerbate negative body image thoughts and help to maintain the binge eating cycle[173].

Gaining appetite awareness is an important step to helping you to take back control of your eating behaviour. This can help you avoid mindless eating, reduce cravings, and identify what your body needs and when.

Just as you have cues for all your needs including sleep, taste, thirst, excretion, and warmth, you were born with hunger, fullness, and satiety signals to enable you to know what your body requires. Over time, you are likely to have learnt to override these instincts whilst being exposed to the cultural messaging that your appetite signals are not to be trusted.

This is especially true if you have experienced a lifetime of dieting. The diet culture narrative emphasises following external rules for eating rather than tuning into and trusting your body's own signals. Appetite is completely subjective and there is no test to determine hunger and fullness levels. Therefore, how can those claiming to be experts accurately know what you as an individual truly need? Furthermore, your appetite naturally fluctuates over hours, days, weeks, and seasons which is entirely normal and to be expected.

Ask yourself why you trust yourself
to meet your needs when you're feeling
thirsty, cold or need the toilet,
but not your appetite

I'm thirsty,
so I'll get a drink

I'm hungry, but
I'll block it out

Satiety is the sense of satisfaction you feel when completing a meal. It is also about the enjoyment and savouring of food. Experiencing physical fullness can trigger anxiety for many people struggling with disordered eating – especially if it's linked to a binge episode. However, you can achieve a satisfying and comfortable sense of fullness without the distress associated with bingeing. It is also worth noting that many people may mistake bloating and digestive issues with the sensation of being overly full. Often what you are really experiencing is gas created by the fermentation of your food when your digestion is not working optimally (as discussed in chapter 22).

Appetite awareness training is really quite simple, but it takes consistency and practice. At first you may find it challenging to locate your hunger cues within your body unless you are extremely hungry or full to the brim. Signs of extreme hunger might be feeling faint, dizziness, stomach growling or gurgling, a feeling of emptiness, or feeling shaky.

When trying to decipher your more subtle signs of hunger before you become ravenous, it's helpful to ask yourself:

How do I know I am hungry?

What are the specific physical cues of my hunger?

You can also ask yourself the same about being satisfied but not overly full:

How do I know I am satiated?

What are the specific physical cues within my body that tell me when to stop eating?

The key is to learn to recognise these physical sensations before you become overly full. Keep checking in with yourself regularly. The subtle hunger and fullness sensations vary from person to person, but I have listed some common ones below.

Subtle signs of hunger include:

- fatigue
- feeling irritable or annoyed
- anxiety or restlessness
- minor stomach pangs
- salivating
- thinking about food or planning your next meal
- losing focus (due to thoughts consistently shifting to food)
- increased attention and interest in the smell of food or the sights and sounds of people eating (including on social media or in a news article)
- difficulty making decisions

Subtle signs of fullness include:

- feeling satisfied without discomfort
- food no longer tastes as good as it did at the beginning of the meal
- slowing down your eating pace
- feeling a sense of contentment

The hunger scale (provided below) is a valuable tool to support you in this process. By rating your hunger on a scale from 0 to 10 before, during, and at the end of your meal, you can begin to identify your physical signs of hunger and satiety.

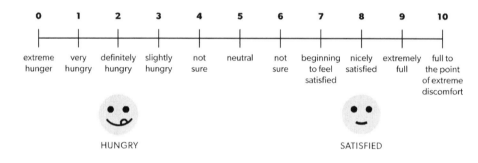

⚡ Action Step

APPETITE AWARENESS

Use the hunger scale below to begin to observe your hunger levels before, during, and after your meal.

Make a note of your appetite rating in your journal before and after each time you eat.

You can download the hunger scale at https://marcellerosenutrition.co.uk/book-resources to keep a copy nearby, such as on your fridge.

Here's how it works:

- Familiarise yourself with different levels of hunger, ranging from 0 to 10, with 0 being extremely hungry and 10 being full to the point of extreme discomfort.

- Take a moment before eating to assess your current level of hunger. Are you at a moderate level of hunger (around 2-3) or are you ravenous (0-1)?

- As you eat, periodically check in with your body to gauge your level of satisfaction and fullness. Aim to stop eating when you are nicely satiated or satisfied

- Observe without judgement – your appetite will vary from day to day and week to week – this is completely normal and not something to fear

Slowing down your eating can really help with this, as you will allow time for your brain to catch up with your stomach.

Please note, as you are at the beginning stage of reconnecting with your appetite, it's extremely important to stick to your regular eating patterns, even if you don't feel hungry at certain times. It takes time to tune in effectively to your body's signals, especially if you have been dieting and overriding your appetite cues for years.

Does the Order You Eat Make a Difference?

Eating certain foods in a particular order might not make a dramatic difference overall, but it can help when you're learning to understand your hunger and fullness signals. Starting with carbs like bread can fill you up quickly, but you might get hungry again soon. On the other hand, proteins, vegetables, and healthy fats take longer to make you feel full but provide longer-lasting energy[174]. So, trying to eat your proteins and veggies first before having carbs may potentially help.

Neurodiversity and Interoception

Interoception is the sensory system that enables you to interpret sensations from within your body. This involves recognising various signals including hunger, fullness, thirst, pain and emotions such as anxiety, sadness, and frustration.

Individuals who are neurodivergent may face extra difficulties in recognising these cues, possibly due to challenges with sensory processing. Specifically, people with ADHD or autism might discover that their eating habits are affected by a decreased sensory awareness, making it more challenging to assess their appetite and practise eating mindfully. If you find this exercise difficult, be kind to yourself, and recognise that repeated daily practice can help.

26. MASTERING MINDFUL EATING

I have witnessed first-hand how the practice of mindful eating has significantly improved my clients' relationships with food, leading to lasting improvements in their eating behaviour. Appetite awareness is just one aspect of this practice.

If you are in the habit of eating while working, using your phone, or watching TV, you may be limiting your body's ability to digest food effectively. Furthermore, eating while distracted or stressed makes it difficult to tune in to your appetite and studies suggest an increased likelihood of overeating and making less helpful food choices.

Since remote working has become more prevalent, I have noticed that people are finding it increasingly difficult to separate their work from their eating habits. This challenge is not exclusive to those who work from home, as even in office settings, it's common for people to work through lunch breaks and eat at their desk.

Consuming foods without distraction, eating with awareness, and taking pleasure from food are some of the key principles of mindful eating. While this way of eating sounds simple, it has become uncommon in today's fast-paced society, where on-the-go eating has become the norm.

How Does Mindful Eating Help?
Researchers have found that eating mindfully enhances satisfaction and reduces the likelihood of ignoring our body's signals that tell us when we are full[175]. Further evidence suggests that when we choose foods based on rigid food

rules, rather than what we truly want, we're more likely to develop persistent cravings[176]. Consequently, this increases the likelihood of succumbing to 'forbidden' foods and the risk of binge eating episodes[177].

A 2018 study found that people who disrupted the process of remembering their meal by watching TV or scrolling on their phone whilst eating showed a higher chance of eating more snacks later, compared to when eating the same amount of food without any distractions. The study concluded that recalling what was eaten during a recent meal prevents further food consumption and plays a part in registering satiety[178].

A separate study found that mindful eating played a critical role in helping participants to effectively manage their cravings and weight without resorting to traditional dieting methods[179].

By being present during your meals, you can also improve your digestive function, minimising bloating and other digestive issues[180] [181]. As a result, this may additionally influence your appetite, increase satisfaction, and reduce your desire to overeat.

☆ Client Story

Maya

Breaking Mindless Eating Patterns

Maya worked as a PR manager in a busy firm and sought my help to overcome her long-standing binge-eating behaviours. Despite numerous attempts at different diets to curb her bingeing, her health had deteriorated significantly. She was experiencing distressing digestive problems, which included constipation, bloating, and acid reflux. Having ruled out any other potential health concerns with her GP, Maya deduced that her eating habits were likely the root cause of her health problems.

Feeling that she had reached breaking point, Maya recognised the need for change. One of the aspects we focused on during our work together was how she ate. Maya confessed to consistently eating mindlessly, whether standing up or in front of the TV, and invariably in haste, whether during a binge episode or not. Afterwards she would always experience intense feelings of shame. Disliking the sensation of feeling overly full, Maya frequently struggled with her constant bloating, a factor that often triggered binge eating episodes.

Maya came to the realisation that a contributing factor to her challenges was her desire to get the process of eating over with as swiftly as possible. When faced with open packets of binge foods, such as crisps or biscuits, she felt compelled to consume them rapidly, 'because then they would be gone'.

Maya began to work on slowing down her eating. She started this process by eating one meal mindfully every day, sitting at a table and incorporating some deep breathing exercises. Initially, the idea of eating without distractions was daunting for Maya, as she preferred not to focus on her food. To address this, I suggested she try listening to a podcast, which proved helpful as it allowed her to maintain a slower pace and savour the textures, flavours, and aromas of her food.

Over time, Maya was both relieved and grateful to find that her digestive problems had improved with less bloating and passing regular stools. Maya began to enjoy eating meals with her partner, actively engaging in conversations which helped to transform her mealtimes into a pleasurable experience. This change, coupled with efforts in other areas, played a significant role in reducing and eventually overcoming her binge eating episodes.

⚡ Action Step

PRACTICE EATING MINDFULLY

Here's how to get started:

1. Choose a meal that you will dedicate to the experience of mindful eating.

   > **TIP:** Taking care with the presentation of your food can be helpful, such as using your best crockery and arranging food on the plate so it looks appetising and appealing.

2. Sit at a table to eat and take some deep breaths to get yourself into the rest and digest state. Now take a moment of appreciation for your food before you eat it. Notice the aroma of the food. Is it making your mouth water?

   > **Note:** If you feel a sense of shame or guilt about eating certain foods, you are likely to be triggering your stress response[182]. Easing the body out of this 'fight or flight' state, before eating, is important for effective digestion and to avoid unhelpful symptoms such as bloating.

3. Ensure you eat your meal without distractions – if you find this difficult, avoid visual distractions such as looking at your TV, computer, or phone and instead try listening to a podcast, the radio, or some music. Try to avoid challenging or uncomfortable conversations during this meal.

4. Take a bite, hold it in your mouth, and pay close attention to what occurs as you begin to chew, notice how the textures change.

5. Take your time. Chew slowly to ensure you have mechanically broken down your food properly before you swallow it. Notice if your eating speeds up and recognise if your eating naturally slows down towards the end of the meal.

Note: Slowing down will allow time for signals to get to the brain and stimulate your digestive enzymes, stomach acid, and muscular contractions before the food arrives. You are also more likely to notice when you are satiated before becoming overly full.

The following may initially help you to slow down your eating:

Put your cutlery down between bites.

Cut the food into very small pieces (This is especially helpful with binge foods)

Eat your food holding the fork in the opposite hand to the usual one

Set yourself the challenge of being the last one to finish if eating with others!

6. Pause during eating to check in with the taste, smell, and texture of your food.

7. Observe any thoughts and feelings that arise about the food or what eating that particular food will lead to, without judgement. Visualise placing unhelpful thoughts on a cloud and watch them float away.

8. Keep checking in with your hunger, fullness, and satisfaction – where are you on the hunger scale?

Once you have done this for one meal, choose the most convenient meal of the day to make this a daily practice. This can then extend to more meals and snacks in due course.

A Mindful Binge

Implementing these tactics can be beneficial in the moment, when faced with a trigger food. If avoiding the urge for binge food proves difficult, eat it slowly and mindfully, break it into small pieces, savour each bite, and try to remain fully present. By doing so, it's likely you'll discover that you have less need for excessive amounts. Mindful bingeing and grazing will slow your eating down, putting *you* back in control, rather than the food.

Free Bonus Resource: Guided Mindful Eating Audio

Before attempting to practice mindful eating on your own, this exercise can serve as a valuable preparatory step. The audio lasts for less than four minutes. Settle into a quiet space where you can sit alone, and bring along a small piece of food – a raisin or something similar is ideal for this.

After completing the exercise, take a moment to reflect on your experience. Consider how you found it, what you discovered, and if you noticed any new or different sensations.

You can access this at: https://marcellerosenutrition. co.uk/book-resources

---

Action Plan Summary

Focus on one action step at a time. Take your time to ensure you feel confident with each step before proceeding to the next one.

Action	What will this help with?	Duration	Chapter	Notes
Increase the variety of plant foods in your diet – use the *30 Plants in a Week* chart and refer to the herbs and spices info sheet	Support your gut microbiome and help balance your appetite hormones	Ongoing, build up using the chart over time	22	
Daily practice to stimulate your vagus nerve. Choose one of the activities to incorporate into your daily routine	To support your nervous system and your gut	Ongoing	23	
Devise your personalised sleep plan. Use the table provided to implement new sleep practices into your daily routine, over time. To prevent overwhelm, avoid attempting to introduce all of these at once.	Help reset your circadian rhythm, improve your sleep, motivation, energy, and help balance your appetite hormones	Ongoing, update as and when needed	24	

Action	What will this help with?	Duration	Chapter	Notes
Appetite awareness training using the hunger scale to observe your hunger levels before and after you eat. Make a note of your appetite ratings in the journal	Reconnect with your hunger and satiety cues	Ongoing	25	
Mindful eating – start with one meal a day	Being present with your food will help with your appetite, cravings, and digestive health	Ongoing	26	

pillar three: think

The way you think has a direct impact on how you feel and, ultimately, your behaviour. In this section you will address your thinking and beliefs about food, dieting, and your body, supported with exercises to help enhance self-awareness and reprogramme your thinking patterns. You will also learn how to tackle ingrained habits and build new, helpful behaviours.

27. YOUR FOOD, BODY AND DIETING MINDSET

It suits diet culture to create a problem for us that needs to be 'solved', lining the pockets of those within the weight loss and diet industry. They strive to instil the deep-rooted belief that we will never be happy, worthy, or loved unless we conform to societal norms of what we should be eating and what a body should look like.

This thinking can become deeply ingrained, leading to an unhappy relationship with food and your body. Ultimately, dieting contributes a great deal in shaping strongly held beliefs that we have about ourselves, food, and eating.

The overarching narrative is that your weight is an issue and the only way to solve it is to keep trying to shrink your body. However, weight loss treatments have low success rates and, if you struggle with emotional or binge eating, pursuing this path only makes matters worse. Research has highlighted (along with my own clinical experience) that addressing the eating behaviours, rather than dieting, is the key element for sustaining weight loss in the long term[183] [184] [185] [186]. Due to this, it's critical to work on healing your relationship with food, rather than simply attempting to lose weight.

Your Thinking Patterns

Your thoughts and beliefs exert a significant influence on your eating behaviour. When it comes to food choices, amounts of food, and forbidden foods, having extreme all-or-nothing thinking patterns plays a role. Your mindset probably includes notions of needing to achieve a specific weight or size to validate your worth, as well as beliefs about how your eating behaviours define you as a person.

Notably, some researchers have discovered that merely thinking about eating forbidden foods can heighten the belief that you will gain weight[187] and, consequently, make you believe you are a *bad* person. However, keep in mind that adopting more constructive thinking patterns can empower you to feel more in control of your eating habits.

In *Nourish*, I delved into the myths surrounding dieting (please revisit chapter 1 to refresh your memory on this). It's important to understand how these misconceptions can cloud your thinking around food and diets, as they have the potential to deeply embed themselves in the core of your belief systems. Let's now explore how these beliefs about food, your body, and yourself give rise to automatic thinking that perpetuates the cycle of emotional eating and bingeing.

Thoughts About Food
Your eating decisions are influenced by factors far beyond hunger or your body's physiological requirements. Food carries profound meaning rooted in your personal and cultural history. It can affect your mood and allows you to express yourself and connect with others.

Your beliefs about food and your body will have begun to form in your early years, with your parents (or caregivers) initially shaping your attitudes and behaviours. As time went on, these foundations will have developed further by the influence of your friends, extended family, and role models. Societal norms will have played a role in your perceptions about food, your body, and the concept of dieting. Presently, with the pervasive impact of social media in our lives, it has become all the more challenging to escape these influences[188].

Once activated, these beliefs will follow a predetermined sequence, operating quietly in the background of your brain, much like a computer programme. However, despite many things changing in your life over time, it is unlikely that your brain's computer programme will receive these updates! While old beliefs serve the purpose of enabling automatic thinking and freeing up mental space for other tasks, the challenge comes when they become unhelpful and outdated. Over time, they can overcrowd your mind, leaving little room for anything else.

The Importance of Your Values

Your belief system also encompasses your values, which play a part in your eating behaviour and emotional response to food. Values provide the foundation for all that we say and do; the things we believe are most important in the way that we live and how we work. For instance, one of your values might be that it is wrong to waste food, or that it is important to eat a healthy diet. Over time, these beliefs develop to mirror the behaviour and thinking of those you are surrounded by, alongside the influence of the food, weight loss, and diet industries. In the course of your life, food may have become linked to reward, punishment, validation, and various other behaviours.

Your Judgements About Food & Eating

According to the *Food Susceptibility Theory*, certain individuals may be more inclined to overeat when food is readily available, especially if there's a moral judgement attached that eating the specific food is bad[189].

Beliefs About Your Capabilities

You also hold beliefs regarding your *ability* to make choices about when, how, and what you eat. These might include thoughts such as *I have no willpower*, or *I'm addicted to sugar*. Perhaps you've spent a lifetime setting intentions that you haven't followed through, resulting in the belief that you simply cannot do it. Many people who emotionally eat or binge believe that they don't have the capability of maintaining a balanced diet for the long term[190].

Some Examples of Unhelpful or Limiting Beliefs:

These are just a few examples, as limiting beliefs can differ from person to person. Overcoming these beliefs involves first recognising them, challenging them, and then reframing them – more on this shortly.

Physical Verses Mental Restriction

It might have surprised you to discover that your efforts to restrict your 'forbidden' foods, calories, or specific food groups may be part of the reason why you feel out of control around food[191].

Some individuals with tendencies toward compulsive eating may go to the extent of avoiding eating altogether, fearing that once they start, they won't be able to stop. In these cases, genuine hunger may evolve into powerful cravings. Ironically, these individuals might be undernourished, wrongly assuming they shouldn't feel hungry because of overeating, when in reality, their brains still need essential nutrients.

However, even if you've now stopped dieting and no longer impose physical restrictions, you might still be practising mental restriction. Mental restriction manifests as feeling shame and anxiety around eating, a lack of peace with food, and denying yourself permission to fully enjoy what you eat. This often results in intrusive thoughts such as *Why am I still hungry?* or *I shouldn't have eaten this; I'm completely out of control.*

Mental restriction presents various challenges. Firstly, these thoughts can significantly impact your emotions and physical sensations. Feeling physically uncomfortable, such as experiencing bloating or anxiety in your stomach, can often trigger more negative thoughts and may even prompt a return to physical restriction.

Secondly, mental restriction often leads to overeating. Research shows that dieters who believe they've consumed their forbidden foods, or more food than they think they should have, often end up eating more, overriding their natural fullness cues[192]. This sets off a perpetual cycle of guilt and overeating.

Finally, mental restriction induces stress within your body. The very act of contemplating restriction triggers the release of stress hormones like cortisol and adrenaline[193]. Your body doesn't differentiate between a genuine threat and a fearful thought before initiating a stress response. Continuous cortisol release can impact not only your weight but also your overall health, with potential repercussions on your digestive system, such as bloating.

It's important to recognise that even if you are incorporating 'forbidden' foods back into your diet, meaningful change will not occur unless there's a shift in your mindset and underlying beliefs.

Your Food Meanings

Looking back to your early years, your parents or other family members may have offered you food for comfort or as a reward. It might be they withheld food as a punishment. Perhaps they insisted you finish everything on your plate before having dessert.

In Western society, food has become so much more than our way of surviving. Everywhere we look around us, on social media, websites, TV, transport ads, we are inundated with the latest health trends and influencer endorsements. Specific foods are associated with particular events including parties, gatherings, or religious festivals. In fact, we are constantly overwhelmed with different foods and different ways to obtain them!

Our society still, to a great extent, dictates that women should be the food providers for the family but remain 'thin' themselves. Food may, for you, bring a sense of conflict on what and how to eat, often leading to feelings of guilt.

Often when we eat, we are expressing how we are feeling, how worthy we are, and how we want to take care of ourselves. It is also about how other people make us feel. Some of my clients admit to finding it stressful to eat out with friends or family. Others find eating alone brings up many emotional connections with food.

Food evokes feelings in pretty much everyone, but research indicates that this effect is even more pronounced among those who perceive themselves as overweight. If you think about losing weight a great deal of the time, there is a greater chance you will comfort-eat in response to having a *bad day*, for example. Moreover, using food as a way to relieve boredom, gain pleasure, or as an emotional support is common for many people.

Have you ever thought about your own personal and unique meanings of food and how they might be influencing your thinking, emotions, and behaviour?

☆ Client Story

Simone

A Turbulent Childhood Influencing Beliefs about Food

Simone had always battled with her relationship with food and felt overwhelmed by her emotional eating struggles. Her internal critical voice constantly bombarded her with thoughts about whether food was good or bad and what she should or shouldn't eat. As part of our work together, we began to explore Simone's food history. Reflecting on her childhood mealtimes, she described them as highly fraught, particularly at home where eating became a source of stress. Simone and her siblings lived in fear of their father's temper. Consequently, she developed a habit of eating quickly to minimise her time at the dinner table and escape the distressing atmosphere.

Food was often withheld as a punishment and treat foods were never available at home. Simone recalls always eating quickly and attempting to sneak food to her room to eat in secret – a habit that continued into her adulthood. Following these secret eating episodes, Simone experienced overwhelming feelings of shame and remorse, leading to further episodes of uncontrolled eating.

By connecting the dots and unravelling her ingrained associations with food, Simone began to challenge and reframe the harmful thoughts that significantly influenced her eating behaviour. This process became a critical element in her journey towards finding peace with food.

⚡ Action Step

FOOD MEANINGS TASK

Use the questions below to help you reflect on your personal relationship with food. Think about your individual food meanings. Do specific foods make you feel good or bad? Try to identify why that might be. Record any insights you have in the space provided below.

Were you forced to eat everything on your plate when you were a child?

Were food shortages around the world discussed?

Were you made to eat food you didn't like?

Were you told not to waste food?

Were you told that specific foods were good or bad for you?

Were you given certain food as treats?

Was there enough food when you were growing up?

Did your parents eat between meals?

Were you given special foods when you were ill?

Did you have any cultural food rituals when growing up?

Did you ever hide or sneak food as a child?

Was food removed as a form of punishment?

Was food given as a treat/way to soothe you as a child?

Did your mum/dad/caregiver enjoy cooking?

Were your parents/caregivers on diets or did they discuss dieting and losing weight?

Did you eat together as a family at mealtimes? What was the atmosphere like? Was there enough time to eat?

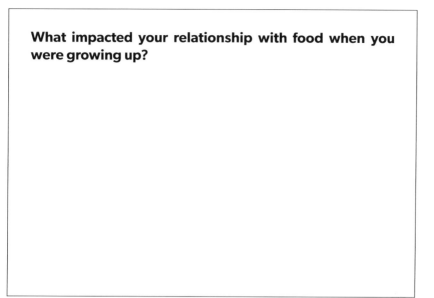

What impacted your relationship with food when you were growing up?

Early Associations with Food, Maintain Eating Behaviours

The reality is that food primarily serves as fuel for your body, supplying the necessary energy and nutrients for its metabolic processes. There is no universal list of *good* or *bad* foods. Any moral judgement about food is a result of cultural conditioning and personal preferences. Contrary to popular belief, food is morally neutral until we layer our opinions on top. In truth, all foods have their place in the context of the 80,000 or so eating experiences we have throughout our lives.

To break free from black-and-white thinking about food, it's essential to unpack the 'baggage' you've attached to different foods. The process will help you to begin approaching your food choices with curiosity, calmness, and flexibility whilst finding satisfaction in what you eat.

⚡ Action Step

SELF-AWARENESS TASK – WHAT YOU TELL YOURSELF ABOUT FOOD

Your food meanings, including early associations and misconceptions, are likely to have influenced the statements you regularly say to yourself. Your next step is to identify and record any personal statements you often tell yourself in the space provided below.

Here are some examples:

I mustn't waste food.

I'll have some sweets to make me feel better.

I hate vegetables.

I feel fat so I must not eat.

Eating any kind of fat makes us fat.

If I skip meals, I will lose weight.

Healthy eating is boring.

Healthy food doesn't taste good.

Weight control is only about calories in and calories out! All calories are the same.

What You Tell Yourself About Food:

⚡ Action Step

FLEXIBILITY EXERCISE

It's likely that, over the years, you've accumulated a lengthy list of rules and regulations regarding food and eating. Adopting flexibility can help you to develop a more balanced and sustainable approach to food[194]. To become more comfortable with breaking your dietary rules, use the space provided below to complete the following exercise. A downloadable version of the task sheet can be found at: https://marcellerosenutrition.co.uk/book-resources

1. List approximately 10 typical behaviours or habits that you consistently do and another list of 10 behaviours or habits that you would never do (These do not need to be food related)

2. Next choose one behaviour from the 'never do' list and try it, and then opt to **not** do one behaviour from the 'usually do' list.

3. How did it make you feel?

4. Did the feeling pass? If so, how quickly?

Once you've completed this exercise once, it can be repeated as you work through some more habits on your list. It's likely that this exercise will make you feel uncomfortable – even if it's something seemingly silly such as putting your socks on first before you get dressed, instead of last. However, it's important to sit with the discomfort and know that it will soon pass.

Here are some examples:

I never wear my watch on my right wrist, tomorrow I will wear my watch on my right wrist

I always check my phone first thing in the morning, tomorrow I'll wait at least an hour

THE BINGE FREEDOM METHOD

Usually Do:	Never Do:
I didn't...	I did...
How it made me feel...	How it made me feel...
Did the feeling pass? How quickly?	Did the feeling pass? How quickly?

28. WHY BODY IMAGE PLAYS A ROLE

It's likely that your beliefs about food are closely tied to your body size, based on the *perceived* power that food has over your appearance. These beliefs also include weight-biased views, such as the idea that people in a larger body should avoid the foods consumed by those in a smaller body. Body size is intertwined with various beliefs about being lucky, successful, attractive, worthy, lazy, and controlled. Have you taken a moment to consider your own body image?

A Note on Body Image

From an early age, we are conditioned to pursue an unattainable ideal of the perfect body size, weight, and shape to define our self-worth[195].

Studies indicate that the vast majority of women over the age of fifty are not satisfied with their body size and shape. These concerning statistics aren't limited to midlife women. Other research shows that as many as 91% of women of all ages and 70% of adolescent girls are also dissatisfied with their body.

Extensive research shows that for many people, their environment when growing up has the biggest impact on how they feel about their body[196] [197]. When the social environment lacks support or is unkind, it can make you feel disconnected from your body, leading to problems like dieting, eating disorders, and relationship issues.

The Pressure to Pursue Thinness at Any Cost

Our society places a premium on small bodies, often prioritising thinness as a symbol of moral superiority and good health. Weight stigma is widespread, leading to discrimination against individuals in larger bodies in various aspects of life. The fear of judgement and rejection is fuelled by diet culture, perpetuated by the media, caregivers, and even healthcare professionals.

For some, dieting and striving for thinness serves as a means to regain control and simplify life. However, this focus on weight can mask underlying stressors that need your attention. Seeking approval from others by altering your body can be tempting, but this validation is typically temporary and often comes from those with their own insecurities.

In order to understand your how your body image evolved and begin to unravel the deep-rooted beliefs you have about your appearance and your worth, it's essential to explore your *body story*.

⚡ **Action Step**

THE BODY STORY TASK

This exercise will help you identify the experiences that formed your body image at various stages of your life[198]. It's probable that you have ignored or forgotten many of these experiences, yet their emotional impact will remain with you.

The objective is to write about these experiences in a clear way, sharing your thoughts and feelings, without blaming yourself or others[199]. Keep in mind that your personal interpretations of the situation, rather than the situation itself, will have shaped your emotional experiences.

Here are the guidelines:

- Dedicate 20 minutes each day for four days (aim to complete this task within a week)

Day 1 = your childhood, Day 2 = puberty and early teens, Day 3 = mid/late teens, Day 4 = adult and recent experiences

- Allow your thoughts to flow without worrying about spelling or grammar
- Choose a quiet, private setting for writing
- Use the first-person perspective. Begin sentences with "I..."
- Incorporate both positive and negative thoughts and feelings
- Try to gain an understanding of how these experiences relate to how you felt about your body and yourself then, and how it affects you now

Bonus Resource
⚡ **Action Step**

BODY IMAGE VISUALISATION

Listen to the guided body image visualisation audio to help reduce body image distress, when needed. You can access this audio at https://marcellerosenutrition.co.uk/book-resources

29. BUILDING SELF-WORTH

Low self-worth doesn't just maintain your eating challenges; it also plays a role in why this behaviour exists in the first place[200]. The shame arising from secret eating is usually only relieved through periods of restraint, and as we know from previous chapters, it is this restraint that contributes to the repetitive binge-restrict cycle.

Low self-worth essentially means you have a low opinion of yourself and believe you are less deserving compared to others. Factors, such as your sense of belonging, identity, and self-confidence, coupled with beliefs about your ability to achieve in life, will influence how you feel about yourself.

Positive self-esteem, on the other hand, includes the belief that you deserve to be loved and treated with respect, where you value your own thoughts, feelings, opinions, and interests[201]. It plays a critical role in determining how you treat yourself. Consequently, building your self-worth is essential for overcoming your challenges with food and your body.

☆ Client Story

Sam

A Self-Esteem and Body Image Breakthrough

Sam was 45 and her self-esteem had hit rock bottom. Sam loathed her appearance and carried a profound sense of shame about her body which compelled her to avoid social events and even forgo holidays. Consequently, various situations had the potential to trigger binge eating events, ranging from trying on clothes, to catching her reflection in the mirror, or seeing herself in photos.

When exploring her body story history, Sam began to recognise the profound influence her early life had had on her body image and self-worth. Sam's mother put her on a diet at the age of 12 after a doctor advised her to lose weight. Her mother frequently made remarks about her own weight struggles and consistently said she was 'bad' for eating certain foods. Sam remembered that she began menstruating earlier than her peers and perpetually felt larger than others, only to later realise it was simply her body undergoing the changes of puberty.

Sam continued to engage in diets, often competing with friends to achieve the lowest weight. As she entered her later teens, periods of restrictive eating culminated in significant binge episodes, leaving her feeling anxious, depressed, and out of control.

We began to address Sam's low self-worth and body image with various exercises which included the task of writing down things that she valued about herself every day. Gradually, as Sam made strides in her eating habits and acknowledged her wins (big and small), Sam developed a growing sense of self-belief in her ability to overcome her challenges. It was during this time that she began to challenge herself to try activities she had previously avoided.

Sam's path towards accepting her body was influenced by the compassion she began to extend to herself, leading to a positive shift in her internal dialogue. She now acknowledged that moving towards body respect would play a key role in self-care and overcoming her eating challenges.

⚡ Action Step

SELF-CARE EXERCISE

When your self-worth is at a low and your mind is cluttered with negative thoughts about yourself and your body, you are far more likely to resort to self-sabotage. It is in these moments that I want you to ask yourself the following question:

"What is the kindest thing I can do for myself right now?"

Then, take action.

This approach is also important whenever you encounter an *'I've blown it'* episode, accompanied by feelings of guilt and shame, or when you are having a *'bad body'* day.

1. Brainstorm some ideas for things that would work for you as acts of kindness, such as a soothing bath with candles, essential oils, or Epsom salts; treating yourself to flowers; establishing a regular time to sit quietly and read; or enjoying a relaxing treatment like a massage. Note: this will be completely individual to you.

2. Carry out an act of kindness for yourself daily for a week.

3. The only requirement is that it should not be earned – it must be a routine part of each day for a week, regardless of whether you've had a 'learning experience' or not, particularly during times when you may be inclined to punish yourself.

⚡ Action Step

SELF-APPRECIATION TASK

- Every day, identify at least one thing that you value about yourself as a person
- Write it down and say it out loud

For example:

I value my ability to be caring to others.

I appreciate that I always try my best.

If you are struggling to find these statements, think about why significant people in your life choose to spend time with you. It might be your energy, wit, or kindness. It may be that you are approachable, conscientious, empathetic, or supportive, for example.

What would others say about your qualities?

⚡ Action Step

ASSERTION PRACTICE

Say the following statements to yourself out loud, as though they are true. Through repeated practice, you will begin to internalise them. The more these statements resonate with you, the more effectively you will be able to take care of yourself[202].

- I can be valued for who I am, irrespective of my body size, weight, or shape.

- If I take care of myself and recognise my own worth, others will do the same.

- I won't deny myself permission to live as fully as people in smaller bodies.

- I may not be what diet culture wants me to believe is the 'perfect size', but I know and do as much as any other person.

- I have the freedom to make food choices, irrespective of my size, weight, or shape.

- I am actively working to transform my eating habits and have made substantial progress.

Can you think of any more powerful statements?

30. THE ART OF SELF-COMPASSION

The idea of self-compassion is frequently misunderstood. It is commonly regarded as self-indulgent, selfish, or a sign of weakness. However, it has the potential to significantly improve your overall well-being[203] and self-esteem, positively influencing your struggles with eating behaviour and body image.[204] [205]

What Exactly is Self-Compassion?

Where compassion is the act of responding to someone's suffering with empathy and understanding, self-compassion refers to how you treat yourself in moments of distress. It is likely you excel at extending compassion to others but struggle when it comes to showing kindness to yourself.

You may fear that without your inner critical voice pushing and punishing you, you might become lazy or give up on yourself. However, it is in fact this inner critic that will erode your self-worth and self-belief and maintain your unwanted eating behaviours.

Research has established a connection between self-compassion and a reduction in binge-eating episodes, improved body satisfaction and enhanced stress coping abilities without resorting to food[206] [207].

31. THE POWER OF YOUR THOUGHTS

As you continue to journal, you may begin to identify various patterns of automatic thoughts.

Much of your eating behaviour will stem from these thoughts, but it is important to note that your thoughts are not facts and need not be accepted as truths. They are opinions, speculations, and assumptions shaped by your personal biases and interpretations, products of your brain's old programming, created in order to fill in the blanks.

Mostly these thoughts will go unnoticed, drifting through your subconscious brain unchecked. Thus, the first step is to become aware of these thoughts, as without noticing them, you cannot do anything about them.

'*I've blown it*' thoughts are perhaps the most common type of automatic thoughts produced when you've deviated from your food rules, often setting off a chain reaction of escalating behaviour[208] [209]. There is a relationship between the situation, subsequent thought, associated feeling, and behaviour that follows[210]. The pattern typically unfolds in this way:

Situation: You break your own food rule by eating some chocolate cake

Thought: I've blown it now so I may as well continue

Feelings: Guilt, shame, frustration, and so on

Behaviour and outcome: You continue to eat/binge on the forbidden food, i.e. your behaviour escalates, reinforcing the belief that you have no self-control

ICEGBERG MODEL

WHAT'S VISIBLE

BEHAVIOUR & EMOTION

e.g. you may have a piece of cake and then feel upset about breaking a 'food rule'

WHAT'S HIDDEN

There are a lot of thoughts feelings and beliefs going on under the surface that influence our behaviours.

Here are just some examples of common feelings, thoughts and beliefs.

If we can start to notice them, we can then challenge them.

NEGATIVE FEELINGS
e.g. guilt, shame, hopelessness

AUTOMATIC THOUGHTS
"I've blown it now so may as well keep eating more cake."

CORE BELIEFS
"I'm unloveable."

ASSUMPTIONS
"If I lose weight, I'll be more loved."

Situation ➤➤➤ automatic thoughts ➤➤➤ feelings that arise ➤➤➤ behaviour and outcome

You may also hold negative **core** beliefs about yourself, such as thinking you are unlovable or flawed. These beliefs can influence how you interpret events, allowing you to view situations through this negative filter. You may resonate with this pattern of thinking:

Example

Core belief: No one will love me

Assumption: If I lost weight, I would be more lovable

Event – you eat chocolate cake ➤➤➤ you interpret it through a core belief filter ➤➤➤ I'm useless and I've failed again ➤➤➤ thought – I need to compensate for the calories ➤➤➤ feeling – guilty ➤➤➤ behaviour – you try to starve for the rest of the day (likely scenario – binge eat in the evening)

However, when you think in a more helpful way, your eating will feel more in control

You eat chocolate cake ➤➤➤ 'I enjoyed it' ➤➤➤ you eat your next meal as normal and get on with your day

---

Are You a Perfectionist?
Perfectionists base their self-worth on their most valued aspects of life, often focusing on controlling their food and weight[211]. If they fail to achieve these standards, it can result in a significant decline in their self-esteem. The first step in moving away from perfectionism is to first become aware of it.

A Note on Selective Attention
Have you ever noticed how you pay more attention to the things that align with what you already believe and ignore those that don't? This is because, with the constant bombardment of stimuli around you, your brain will naturally filter and prioritise what it thinks is important.

However, this is not always helpful. For instance, if you hold the belief that you are a failure, you'll notice everything that's not right in your life and ignore the positive things you do well.

This tendency can intensify your problems, as they become the sole focus of your attention. When you repeatedly tell yourself that you are a failure, it becomes a belief, shaping your perspective to see only the negative aspects. Consequently, whatever you selectively attend to becomes magnified, feeling like an overwhelming problem.

This phenomenon is relevant to anyone who has ever been on a diet, as the more you attempt not to think about food, the more it occupies your thoughts[212].

⚡ Action Step

COGNITIVE REFRAMING

Reframing a thought does not mean changing it to a positive statement that you do not believe; rather, it involves subtly altering how you perceive the situation itself. It is a skill that requires time and awareness before you can successfully shift your thinking, but it is achievable.

The process will help you to recognise outdated, unhelpful beliefs, allowing you to create new ones that align with what is happening now – think of it as upgrading your brain's computer programme!

Here's how to get started:

1. Use the worksheet below to document your unhelpful, automatic thought. Begin by writing '*I notice that I'm thinking...*' rather than writing the thought as if it were a fact. Writing the thoughts down will help to bring them to the surface.

2. Note down the circumstances that triggered the thought.

Then question whether the thought provides the best interpretation of the current situation and identify a more realistic alternative – Ask yourself, *what could be a more useful way of thinking? What can I say to myself instead? Can I imagine a way to think about this that would serve me better?* Write it down.

Finally, record any changes in outcome or shifts in how you feel.

Repeat this process over several weeks. Over time, challenging your old beliefs will become easier, and the new, helpful thoughts will gradually replace your previous beliefs.

(You can access a downloadable version of this worksheet at: https://marcellerosenutrition.co.uk/book-resources)

The Unhelpful Automatic Thought

I notice that I'm thinking

The Situation

Your New Perspective (i.e. The Reframed Thought)

Changes in Feelings or Outcome?

Here's an example:

The Unhelpful Automatic Thought
I notice that I'm thinking I overate, so I'm skipping the next meal to make up for all those calories

The Situation
Went to a party where a lunch buffet was served

Your New Perspective (The Reframed Thought)
Eating dinner will stop me craving and bingeing and keep me nourished.

Changes in Feelings or Outcome?
I feel slightly less anxious and the evening didn't end in a binge!

TIP: When you experience critical thoughts, such as assuming what others might be thinking about you, ask yourself:

Is this really true?

How much do I believe that it is?

What is the evidence to support it?

What is the evidence against it?

Examples of how to reframe unhelpful thoughts:
This is a 'learning experience'

Everyone makes mistakes, I approve of myself

I notice I am beating myself up, I will not do that any more

Next time I have those cravings I will do something different first

Slipping up is part of recovery, I am learning how to manage this

I approve of the fact I took some steps to break my behaviour pattern

What is the kindest thing I can do for myself right now?

I am learning and will be able to cope with this situation better next time

Having Trouble Recognising Unhelpful Thoughts?
It can help to revisit the triggering event by closing your eyes and mentally replaying it frame by frame to uncover the associated thoughts. Ask yourself, "What was going through my mind at that moment? What did I tell myself?" Then record the initial thought that comes to your mind.

For example:

Triggering event: Getting ready for a party

I was looking for something to wear

I then tried on my favourite pair of jeans that I hadn't worn for a while

They were too tight

Associated thought: *I will never look nice*

I might as well just eat that pack of biscuits

Outcome: Has a binge later

⚡ Action Step

REFRAME UNHELPFUL THOUGHTS IN YOUR JOURNAL PAGES
You can continue the practice of reframing unhelpful thoughts by making a note of them in your journal pages – especially when there has been a Learning Experience.

Use the same technique as above, noting the situation, the thought (beginning it with, *I notice I am thinking...*), and then reframe the thought.

TIP: If you find it challenging to reframe a thought, consider viewing it as if it was something your best friend or someone you care deeply about was saying to themselves.

What would you say to them in that situation?

It's important you offer the same compassion to yourself as you would a loved one.

ADHD Mindset

If you have ADHD, you may be particularly susceptible to persistent, unhelpful thoughts and find yourself stuck in rumination, especially with situations that create a strong emotional reaction. These can take up a lot of brain space. The key is to try to observe what's going on without judgement.

A helpful technique is to visualise these unhelpful thoughts or loops of thoughts sitting on a cloud and gently floating away.

32. HELPFUL HABITS?

Just as it is possible to modify unhelpful thinking, you also have the power to change problematic habits and create new, more helpful behaviours. Breaking habits can be challenging because they are deeply ingrained within your neural pathways.

Think of habits like the superhighways of your brain. Each time you try to establish a new behaviour it feels arduous, like crossing a field of long grass. However, with consistent repetition, your journey along the same route forms a narrow path and gradually widens, until it becomes your new superhighway. Forming a new habit feels much the same, at first it feels like hard work, and you must repeat it consistently to embed it. New habits need to be kept as simple as possible and tended to as small, doable changes which can be built upon. It can also be beneficial when a new habit is linked to an established habit, such as doing 5 minutes of stretching straight after cleaning your teeth when you get up in the morning.

Changing your habits may also be challenging because of the values linked to certain behaviours. It's not just about doing things differently; it involves changing how you perceive situations. This includes beliefs about the habit itself and your self-efficacy beliefs related to the behaviour – in other words, believing that you can do this.

The process of change is explained simply in four stages[213]. At first, you are usually unaware of an unhelpful behaviour. By the second stage, you are becoming aware but are not yet doing anything about it. By the third stage, you begin to change the behaviour. This will take effort on your part, and you may not always be successful in making different choices[214]. Reaching the fourth stage means that you have successfully changed your behaviour without having to think about it or try hard.

THE 4 STAGES OF HABIT CHANGE

STAGE 1	STAGE 2	STAGE 3	STAGE 4
You are unaware of your unhelpful behaviour	You have become aware of your unhelpful behaviour but haven't done anything about it yet	You begin to change your behaviour but have to work quite hard at it	Your behaviour has changed without having to think about it

---

☆ **Client Story**

Breaking Behaviour Patterns and Forming New Habits

Lucy, aged 28, was a stressed accountant working in a large finance company. She commuted daily into the city and worked long hours.

Lucy's typical routine involved fasting until lunch, then grabbing a bagel to eat at her desk, and finding herself grazing from mid-afternoon onwards. There was a vending machine near where she sat containing crisps and crackers, and biscuits were regularly passed around the office, which only fuelled her snacking habits. On her way home, Lucy would stop to buy a chocolate bar and Diet Coke to "keep her going", resulting in little appetite for dinner by the time she arrived home. Her evenings were spent watching TV, snacking on the sofa or in bed.

Lucy had been so focused on her career that her eating habits hadn't bothered her at first. However, recently, she became aware of skin problems in addition to a significant decline in her energy levels, impaired concentration, and disrupted sleep, resulting in a constant feeling of grogginess and fatigue each day.

When looking at her behaviour patterns, we were able to identify the specific habits that needed addressing. Lucy therefore worked on the following:

- Incorporating breakfast in the morning to maintain balanced blood glucose levels and provide energy.
- Choosing between bringing a nutritious packed lunch to work or buying a balanced option, to reduce her afternoon slump and cravings, and also giving herself a 15-minute walk.
- Carrying a helpful snack with her for the journey home. (She was no longer craving snacks at the office after her nourishing lunch.)
- Planning and preparing balanced evening meals in advance, using a food subscription box a few times a week to save time.
- Ensuring snacks were only eaten at the kitchen table (eating them slowly and mindfully) while reserving the sofa for watching TV and the bed for sleep.

Lucy managed to implement each of these changes, addressing them slowly, one by one. Over time, she began to notice that her skin had improved, she had more energy, and could concentrate better. She also was surprised to observe that her cravings had largely disappeared, and she even enjoyed undisturbed sleep.

TIP: If your habit is always reaching for biscuits whenever you watch TV, for example, you can try to consciously eat a biscuit at the kitchen table before turning your programme on or make yourself a hot drink instead.

Whether you catch yourself at the time, before, or after the event, make a note of this in your journal. Again, this must be an observation, **not** a reason to berate yourself.

A helpful method for recognising your unwanted habits involves exploring your habit cycle[215]. This entails considering the triggers that initiate the habit, the behaviour itself, and the underlying benefit or need you're trying to satisfy.

YOUR HABIT CYCLE

BEHAVIOUR
what unhelpful foods
do you go for?

TRIGGER
environment,
time of day,
stressful situation,
person, etc.

NEED
e.g. comfort immediately
after eating the food

BUT...
how does it make
you feel five
minutes later?

⚡ Action Step

Use the Habit Cycle template below to identify your personal behaviour patterns. (Print out a downloadable version of this at: https://marcellerosenutrition.co.uk/ book-resources)

The Trigger

This could be a particular location, emotional state, time of day, stressful experience, or person. Here are some examples:

You are starving after work and walk past the cake shop every day on your way home

Your partner has made you angry

You are watching TV in the evening

You are feeling lonely and or bored – no one is around, nothing to do

You have an uncomfortable conversation with a family member on the phone which makes you feel anxious

You come home from a stressful day at work and feel deserving of a treat

The Behaviour
Next look at the specific behaviour that the trigger typically leads to:

What would you buy, or seek out?

Where would you get it from? E.g., your cupboard/fridge/ at the petrol station?

What foods do you go for at this point without thinking about it?

Make a note of the 'behaviour' that regularly follows the trigger you have noted down.

How would you eat it?

Benefit or Need
Now consider what you want the behaviour to give you:

What benefit are you expecting from it, or need are you trying to meet?

It maybe comfort, relief, excitement.

You may be exhausted and need an energy boost.

It is likely that you need something to help you cope with uncomfortable emotions such as loneliness, boredom, anxiety, or sadness.

The automatic thoughts that follow
Perhaps a few hours or even minutes later, the negative, automatic thoughts kick in, such as:

'Why did I do that?'

'I've failed again'

'I've blown it'

'I'm rubbish'

'Why can't I stop it?'

'I'm an awful person

These can often provide a trigger for more impulsive eating, and so the cycle continues.

How can you break the cycle?

Once you have identified the cycle, it's time to reflect on what you can do about it. There may be an opportunity to avoid the trigger by doing something differently. However, this may not be feasible if the situation is beyond your control, such as dealing with a stressful workplace situation. In this case, look at the behaviour itself. If you always walk the same way home past a tempting cake shop, could you change your route? Similarly, if your routine involves buying chocolate at the petrol station after a stressful day, could you refuel at a different time or when you feel more emotionally stable?

Next, turn your attention to the benefit or need. Could you change the coping mechanism or find a different way to soothe yourself? You can pre-empt this situation in advance by brainstorming a few go-to, non-food-related rewards or self-soothing techniques that resonate with you. This could be anything from gifting yourself a quiet time to read, a relaxing bubble bath, or creating artwork. (We will cover self-soothing techniques further in chapter 40.)

Often the *benefit* of the unwanted behaviour is short-lived and it's likely that unhelpful thoughts will follow. These automatic thoughts are damaging – corroding how you value yourself, decreasing your motivation and the belief that you can overcome this. (At this point, it's important to reframe these thoughts and prevent the cycle from continuing.)

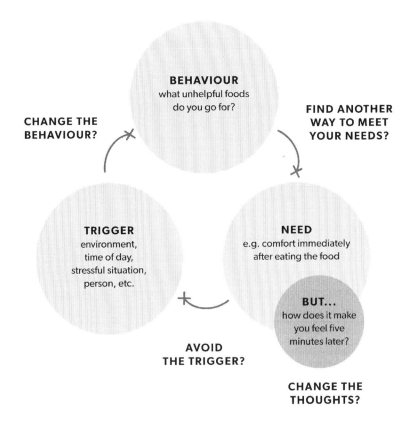

⚡ Action Step

IF-THEN STATEMENTS

Conditional *if-then* statements provide a technique you can use to anticipate any repetitive triggers that might lead to an unwanted eating episode. You can prepare for these situations by brainstorming three possible actions you'll take. Try them out to see which one works best.

This approach enables your rational brain to assert control over old, automatic behaviours.

For example:

*If I go out with my friends tomorrow, **then** I will have a small snack beforehand to prevent me becoming overly hungry.*

Are Second Helpings a Habit When You're Full?

Are you in the habit of continuing to eat after your meal, when already full? Perhaps you go back for a second helping because it is there. Or maybe you continue to graze on food, or binge after your meal.

The behavioural satiety sequence (BSS)[216] is a theory that outlines the natural progression of behaviours seen in animals before, during, and after eating.

An example of this is the transition from eating, to activity such as grooming after a meal. Studies show that adopting this pattern can be beneficial for humans too. Specifically, planning a half hour activity after eating allows your body to signal fullness, reducing the desire to overeat.

In order for this to work it needs to be:

- Pre-planned and something you can easily go and do straight away
- Non-food related and away from where you keep your food
- Something that uses your hands and engages your mind (think painting, knitting, arts and crafts, puzzles, and the like)
- An activity lasting at least thirty minutes to give your mind ample time to register its fullness signals

By repeating this daily, it has the potential to develop into a constructive new habit.

Action Plan Summary

Focus on one action step at a time. Take your time to ensure you feel comfortable with each step before proceeding to the next one.

Action	What will this help with?	Duration	Chapter Reference	Notes
Food Meanings Task	Use the questions provided to help you to reflect on what has influenced your relationship with food over time.	One-off exercise	27	
Self-Awareness Task – What You tell Yourself about Food	Identify and record any personal statements you often tell yourself about food	One-off exercise	27	
Flexibility Exercise	Use the table provided to help improve your flexibility around food and eating. Helps reduce rigidity around breaking food rules	2-4 weeks	27	
Body Story Task	Reflect on what has influenced your beliefs about your body to help unravel them and work towards body respect and acceptance	One-off exercise	28	
Bonus Resource:Body Image Visualisation	To help reduce body image distress. Available at: https://marcellerosenutrition.co.uk/book-resources	When needed	28	
Self-Care Exercise	Do something kind for yourself daily for a week and especially after a *Learning Episode*, or when you are having a *bad body* day. This will help to build your self-worth and mental resilience.	Initially for one week and then as and when required	29	

Self-Appreciation Task	Identify what you value about yourself as a person to help improve your self-worth	Daily – ongoing	29	
Assertion Practice	Practise the statements provided daily to develop your resilience and improve self-worth	Daily – ongoing	29	
Cognitive Reframing	Use the worksheet provided to become aware of your unhelpful, negative thoughts and reframe them to shift your mindset, improving self-esteem and resilience.	3-6 weeks	31	
Thought Work in Your Journal Pages	Continue to reframe your unhelpful thoughts by making a note of them in your journal pages, to shift your mindset, improving self-esteem and resilience.	Ongoing	31	
Habit Cycle Task	Use the Habit Cycle template to help you build new habits and let go of old, unwanted behaviours.	Until you have identified your key habit cycles	32	
If-then statements	Brainstorm three possible actions you'll take. Try them out to see which one works best.	Helps to anticipate and prepare for repetitive triggers	32	

pillar four: feel

This final pillar is focused on understanding the impact of your emotions on your eating habits. You'll gain insights into regulating difficult feelings and develop new, more helpful coping mechanisms. You will discover how to manage your cravings and how they are connected to your feelings, while also building new boundaries and harnessing appropriate support from the loved ones in your life.

33. MANAGING FEELINGS WITH FOOD

Many people turn to food as a way to manage their emotions[217]. However, when these emotions are negative and intertwined with thoughts of not being good enough or greedy, for example, they can feel intense and overwhelming. Eating may then become a way to shut out or numb these feelings.

It may be that using food to soothe has developed into a learned response to prolonged stress over the years. In the early stages of your life, if food was readily available, it may have offered comfort during periods of stress. Conversely, if food was not freely available during your childhood, your tendency might be to stock up on 'treat' foods now. It might be that you rely on food to provide you with a sense of safety and stability if important people in your life have let you down. Ultimately, eating may have evolved into a way of rewarding yourself, without addressing your genuine needs.

Food provides immediate gratification, often serving as a distraction from your emotional state. You may feel momentarily better because of the pleasurable experience of eating food that tastes good, coupled with an elevation in brain chemicals. However, using food to cope may be preventing you from recognising and processing your emotions, which is an essential step in freeing yourself from binge and emotional eating.

Has this ever happened to you?
Has something made you **feel** angry, sad, stressed, or anxious?

Leading to the **thought** – *I can't handle feeling like this*

Leading to the **behaviour** – Standing at the kitchen cupboard eating a pack of biscuits

Leading to **feelings** of guilt and shame

…and the cycle continues…

Food evokes emotions in pretty much everyone, but research suggests even more so if you are in a larger body. For those who think about losing weight much of the time, there is a greater chance they will comfort-eat in response to having a 'bad day', for example.

34. UNMASKING YOUR EMOTIONS

It's a widespread experience for those with disordered eating behaviours to struggle to recognise and feel a full range of emotions, particularly the negative ones. The inclination to sidestep these feelings often stems from the discomfort they bring.

However, feelings are not right or wrong, and confronting and embracing uncomfortable feelings can help you to build emotional resilience and offer valuable insight into the underlying causes of your eating behaviour. Here's how to get started:

⚡ Action Step

LABELLING YOUR FEELINGS

Use the *Feelings Chart* to identify and name your feelings. This will help you to broaden your emotional vocabulary and handle difficult feelings more effectively. Record these emotions in your journal pages and especially before and after a *Learning Experience*.

FEELINGS CHART

HAPPINESS	
overjoyed	triumphant, ecstatic, delighted
cheerful	merry, pleased, amused, buoyant
content	satisfied, mellow, serene
relieved	safe, grateful, reassured, unburdened, appreciative
proud	important, confident, slef-assured, smug, haughty
loving	tender, compassionate, affectionate
SURPRISED	
startled	shocked, dismayed, horrified
confused	disconcerted, perplexed, stunned, baffled
amazed	astonished, bewildered, dumbfounded
SAD	
hopeless	miserable, powerless, dejected, despairing, defeated
depressed	gloomy, sombre, empty, deflated, downcast
lonely	detached, outcast, lost, grief-stricken, mortified
guilty	remorseful, ashamed, humiliated, embarrassed, mortified
abandoned	unwanted, deserted, rejected, unloved, inadequate
bored	apathetic, indifferent, disinterested
FEARFUL	
scared	unsettled, afraid, terrified, alarmed, shaken
worried	uneasy, nervous, apprehensive, concerned
anxious	panicky, distressed, tense, fretful
insecure	unsafe, suspicious, vulnerable, unsure, weary
ANGRY	
mad	furious, enraged, vengeful, livid
annoyed	irritated, tetchy, resentful, incensed
distant	withdrawn, aloof, standoffish
aggressive	hostile, confrontational, provocative
critical	intolerant, frustrated, impatientm 'I've blown it'
disgusted	repulsed, loathing, disappointed, horrified
threatened	exposed, jealous, vulnerable
hurt	devastated, crushed, offended, insulted, slighted
hateful	resentful, bitter, violated, scornful

⚡ Action Step

SELF-COMPASSION TASK

Chapter 31 guided you to challenge negative thoughts by reframing them with the help of your new food and body wisdom. To complete this process, use the journal pages to incorporate a compassionate statement that feels empathetic and comforting. Don't forget to reinforce this practice by revisiting the self-care exercise highlighted in chapter 29.

Here are some examples of what might come up in your food journal:

Labelling your feelings

I'm feeling guilty for eating 'all that' lunch.

Compassionate Statements

Eating lunch will keep my blood glucose balanced.

It's okay to feel guilty, nothing will happen.

Self-Care

What's the kindest thing I can do for myself right now and how can I resolve this emotion?

Listen to some music.

Labelling your feelings

I'm feeling angry as I ate 'too many' nuts.

Compassionate Statements

Eating this as a snack will help to keep me satiated.

It's okay to feel annoyed, nothing will happen.

Self-Care

What's the kindest thing I can do for myself right now and how can I resolve this emotion?

Go for a short walk.

Riding the Wave of the Emotion

Experiencing negative emotions is a common part of life, and it is natural to want to make them go away. Nonetheless, do not underestimate the importance of learning to 'sit' with the discomfort, which will help to reduce the intensity of the emotion and allow it to subside.

Rather than judging a negative feeling or struggling against it, sitting with your emotion involves allowing yourself to express it safely and gently. You can do this by identifying the feeling (as explained earlier in the chapter) and begin to notice physical bodily sensations associated with the feeling. (I will explain the defusion technique in the following chapter, to illustrate how to do this.) Slow down and be patient with yourself, and try viewing the feeling as valuable information, rather than something to fear.

It can help by visualising your emotion as if you are surfing a wave. Although the intensity will rise, it will reach a peak and eventually dissipate. Know that the feeling is transient and won't last for long[218].

35. CONQUERING YOUR CRAVINGS

Do you view your cravings as a weakness? They are, in fact, signs or signals that need your attention. The *Cravings Quiz* serves as a tool to help you identify what these signals may mean when you have a craving for a specific food.

Defusion is a powerful technique that can help you to unravel your thoughts and emotions, allowing for effective self-soothing and acceptance of your cravings[219] [220] [221]. This will reduce anxiety about whether to give in to the craving or not and is associated with a significant reduction in binge events.

The *Delay Response* strategy is another effective method for managing cravings. Each of these is explained further in the boxes below.

⚡ **Action Step**

CRAVINGS QUIZ
- Consider first, are you genuinely hungry?
- Would it help to have something different to eat?
- What is going on with you physically right now?
- Are you tired/unwell/premenstrual?
- Did you eat trigger food/drink alcohol?
- What are you really wanting?
- What else will help?
- Is there something you're not saying?
- Or an emotion you're not recognising?
- Are you lonely/anxious/stressed or the like?
- What has happened that might have caused these feelings?

Refer to the *Cravings Quiz* as often as possible when you experience an intense desire for a particular type of food.

⚡ Action Step

DELAY RESPONSE

When faced with a strong urge to binge, take a moment to pause and remind yourself that you have the control, not the food, and that you can eat that food whenever *you* choose. Then tell yourself that you choose to have the food in 20 minutes' time (or anywhere from 5 to 30 minutes). Then leave the room and do something else. After that time, you'll likely find that the intensity of the craving has diminished.

If you do decide to return to the food you crave after that time, eat it with intent. Sit down, eat slowly, and stay fully present in the experience. You may start to eat and realise you don't want it all and can therefore choose to stop.

One of the challenges of this technique is recognising the urge to binge, which can be so automatic that you are not really conscious of it. However, over time and with consistent practice, you can rewire your brain and make this new response more natural.

⚡ Action Step

DEFUSION

Given that emotions manifest as physical sensations in the body, defusion provides a means to identify where you feel them, enabling you to observe and acknowledge challenging feelings without becoming overwhelmed. Defusion is a valuable strategy that must be practised regularly to become effective. It will help you to create space between your internal experiences and your reaction to them.

The more frequently you practise this exercise the more effective it will be.

Defusion for Cravings

When faced with a craving, start by referring to the *Cravings Quiz*. Then pause and apply the following strategy to weaken your craving:

1. Recognise you are having an intense craving.
2. Become aware of the physical sensations that this reaction brings to your body.
3. Repeat the statements, provided below, to yourself, tailoring them to address your specific cravings, thoughts, and sensations.

I notice I am having a craving

I notice that the craving is in my mouth

My mouth is watering and I'm seeing the picture of the food I want to eat

My heart is beating and I'm saying 'I want it now'

I notice I'm quarrelling with myself and no one's going to stop me

(OR I notice I'm quarrelling with myself – I want it – You shouldn't)

I notice this is causing me anxiety

(Take a deep breath in)

I accept all of this in this moment

(Breathe out)

Thank you, mind

At this point, the intensity of the craving should have diminished. Distance yourself from the food and engage in a different activity to divert your attention – refer to the Delay Response technique above.

<u>**Defusion for Managing Difficult Emotions**</u>

The first step is to recognise you are having an emotional reaction. Become aware of the physical sensations that this reaction brings to your body. Repeat the statements, provided below, to yourself, tailoring them to address your specific thoughts, feelings, and sensations.

I notice that I'm having a big emotional experience

I notice that I'm feeling anxious

I notice that my heart is racing and I'm shaking

I notice that I can feel it in my chest

(Take a deep breath in)

I accept all of this in this moment

and then breath out

Thank you, mind

Does it feel any better? (e.g. heart rate slowing)

What did you learn or notice?

Managing Trigger Foods in Your Home

Dealing with foods in your home that trigger binge behaviour can be challenging. Here are some factors to consider:

- Avoid keeping binge trigger foods in your home. This may not be possible if they are purchased by or for others. Consider whether having trigger foods at home is a genuine necessity or a self-imposed belief.

- Store binge trigger foods in less visible or accessible places, such as on high shelves or in opaque containers. It can sometimes be helpful if they are kept out of sight! If these foods are kept at home for others, ask for help from your partner to support you with this.

- Stock your home with more helpful alternatives, such as switching your regular chocolate for dark chocolate which is less likely to be triggering. Having nutritious snacks readily available can help satisfy your cravings.

- Recognise that complete avoidance of trigger foods may not be a sustainable solution. Over time, I recommend intentionally buying a small quantity of a trigger food and giving yourself permission to eat it. However, it must be eaten mindfully. Choosing to eat these foods in the company of others can often alleviate the shame linked with eating them thereby decreasing the likelihood of binge eating.

- Practise mindful eating practices when you choose to have trigger foods at home. Remind yourself of the mindful eating techniques outlined in chapter 26 for guidance on how to do so.

36. DEALING WITH 'BAD BODY' DAYS

Have you ever wondered why you feel relatively okay about your body one day, only for your anxiety to soar the next because the scales tell a different story? The reality is that your body does not change dramatically from one day to the next. While the scales may suggest you've gained weight, the fact is that your weight can fluctuate every day for various reasons which have nothing to do with what you've eaten.

Experiencing a *bad body day* is common among people of all body sizes, regardless of their weight. For some of us, a bad body day reinforces feelings of body dissatisfaction and compulsions to control weight and eating.

This sensation or feeling that we are having a bad body day can be triggered by bloating, particularly when clothing feels tight around the waist, along with other changes in physical sensations such as increased fullness. However, buried emotions can also intensify feelings of body dissatisfaction. It is therefore important to check in with yourself and ask what else you are feeling and thinking and then address it directly by referring back to the *Feelings Chart* and the *Body Image task* below to help with this.

☆ Client Stories

'Bad body' day triggers

Wendy used to weigh herself obsessively. If the scales didn't show a decrease, she'd panic and tell herself that she had failed again. This would consistently lead to her restricting her food for the entire day, leading to evening binge eating.

Jenny felt uncomfortable in every outfit she tried on before an event. This led to thoughts 'Nothing fits me, I look disgusting, I am disgusting'. She turned to food for comfort to cope with her distress.

Ellie would actively avoid being in photos whenever she could, because she felt terrible about her body. When Ellie saw herself in family photos from a recent gathering, it fuelled her distress, causing her to despise her body more. Later that evening, when the kitchen was empty, she resorted to bingeing on whatever she could find as a response to her emotional distress.

Reminder: Revisit the self-care exercise outlined in chapter 29. What kind gesture can you gift yourself on a *bad body day* instead of punishing yourself by restricting food or compulsively eating?

⚡ Action Step

BODY IMAGE TASK

Have you ever considered just how much your weight and body size matter to you? When you think about your body, what emotions do you feel? What do you do or not do because of beliefs about your body?

Each situation or event that provokes body image distress brings its unique set of automatic thoughts, emotions, and behaviours. Identifying the unique components of each episode increases your awareness and empowers you to potentially change your responses to challenging situations.

Remember, you may not be able to change the situation, but you do have the power to change your reaction to it.

Here's an example:

What was the triggering event or situation?

E.g. *Went to a party where everyone one was really slim and attractive.*

What did you think about yourself and your body?

I kept thinking I looked so big and frumpy compared to the other women there. I wished I could hide. I thought that everyone else was thinking, She looks awful. *I kept thinking, I can't eat anything or they will think I'm just greedy. I thought about not eating for the next few days.*

What emotions did you feel and where in the body did you feel it (use the Feelings Chart and Defusion strategy)?

Upset, angry at myself, self-conscious, envious. I was sweating and my heart was beating faster.

How did this affect your behaviour (e.g. start a new diet, comfort-eat, binge-eat)?

I didn't talk much to anyone. I didn't eat anything. I left the party early and binged when I got home.

Complete the exercise below, initially reflecting on your feelings during a recent episode of body image distress. (A printable version of this worksheet can be downloaded at: https://marcellerosenutrition.co.uk/book-resources)

What was the triggering event or situation?

What did you think about yourself and your body?

What emotions did you feel and where in the body did you feel it (use the Feelings Chart and Defusion strategy)?

How did this affect your behaviour (e.g. start a new diet, comfort-eat, binge-eat)?

Now, shift your focus to observing a current episode as it unfolds using the worksheet below. This includes an additional section for recording more helpful alternative thoughts, such as:

- I am not succumbing to the diet culture idea of a perfect body size
- No one is perfect, everyone has imperfections and that is normal
- I don't need to beat myself up because I am not the same size or weight as some other people

Note: Your statements about what you appreciate about yourself (see chapter 29) will be helpful here

What was the triggering event or situation?

What did you think about yourself and your body?

What thoughts would serve me better?

More Body Image Tasks
~Curate your social media feed

Remove diet content and influencers who endorse diets and replace them with body acceptance, body diverse and non-diet accounts.

~Give away clothes that no longer fit you or feel comfortable

If possible, purchase some new clothes that you feel good in. Try online shopping, new or second-hand, if you don't enjoy trying on in the store.

~Body Image Ladder

Draw a ladder. Place the body part that causes you the least anxiety and you least despise at the bottom, and work your way up to the body part that causes you the most distress.

Now, beginning at the bottom, think about that specific body part and practise any of your relaxation or breath work techniques. (See chapter 40 for ideas.) Continue until you get to the top.

~Write a letter of appreciation to your body[222]

Include everything you appreciate about the functionality of each part of your body and all that it does for you.

E.g. *Thank you for my eyes that allow me to see the colourful flowers in my garden, I appreciate my stomach which has enabled me to carry and give birth to my child,* and so on.

37. REDEFINING HAPPINESS

When I first ask clients why they want to create change in their life, the answers often revolve around familiar themes: "I want to lose weight", "I want to be healthy", or "I want to lose weight to become healthier". What I really want to understand is **why** *do you want to lose weight?*

You will be able to uncover your true 'why' when you peel away the layers of your motivations and look deeper. This is an important exercise, as your surface level motivations may include wanting to fit into a certain dress size or please societal expectations, but the true motivations that will drive you to create change are likely to go far beyond the number on the scales.

Is It about your Health?

It is possible to improve your health without shrinking your body[223]. Healthful behaviours, such as eating in a balanced way, improving sleep, reducing stress, and gently moving your body will all help to create physiological change within the body without the need to shed pounds.

Contrary to popular belief and the narrative of many medical professionals, being in a smaller body doesn't automatically equate to better health[224]. I have worked with many individuals in lower BMI ranges who struggle profoundly with their health. Many of them experience exhaustion, low mood, and a range of health issues, including hormonal imbalances, skin problems, digestive issues, and thinning hair among others. Conversely, there are many people in larger bodies who have excellent health and healthy blood test results to show for it[225].

A Note on BMI

BMI (body mass index) was originally developed by a statistician for studying populations and trends, not for assessing individual health. Despite its limitations, it was later adopted for this purpose[226].

BMI has several flaws. It does not distinguish between muscle and fat. Individuals with a higher proportion of muscle may have a high BMI despite low body fat, and pregnancy can also skew BMI. An understanding of where fat is distributed around your body, such as visceral fat around the organs, offers a more accurate measure of health than BMI[227].

People labelled 'overweight' (BMI of 25+) or 'obese' (BMI of 30+) are consistently told to lose weight to improve their health. However, several studies have found that being in the overweight category can have a protective effect. Many individuals within the 'healthy' BMI range are not healthy, and those below the healthy range often face significant health issues. Studies show that as BMI decreases below the normal range, mortality increases[228].

Many people ultimately seek change because they believe it will make them happier. They hope that by shedding pounds, they'll find contentment. If you've experienced a smaller body in the past, be honest with yourself about whether you were genuinely happy then. For some, the answer is no. It was never about the weight; it was about finding happiness.

It is possible that you were indeed happy, but that happiness may have been short-lived, and the pursuit of thinness continued because you were never satisfied. Perhaps it was because you received external validation, from others, perhaps from individuals dealing with their own food and body challenges. Reflecting on aspects of your life during that time, such as your relationship or job satisfaction, may reveal that being thinner wasn't the true source of your happiness.

Consider what it is you genuinely want in life. Is it happiness, calmness and freedom around food, boundless energy, a sense of worthiness, or the mental space to pursue your passions? If so, that is your true 'why'.

Re-Evaluating Your Eating Behaviour

Armed with this understanding, you might question whether dieting, control, and restriction align with what you truly want. Will they lead you to your authentic 'why', or are there more effective ways to achieve what you really want?

While you question this, always bear in mind that if nothing changes, nothing will change!

Knowing Your Values – What is Important to You?

Your values serve as the guiding principles that shape your decisions, actions, and priorities. Whether you are aware of it or not, you spend an extensive amount of your mental and emotional energy protecting, maintaining, and living out your values. It's important to ensure that your goals are aligned with your values and that there is no conflict between them.

Your values provide a solid foundation for discovering your true 'why'. Identifying them enables clarity, resilience, behaviour consistency, boundary setting, and healthier relationships.

⚡ Action Step

VALUES EXERCISE

Identify and record your top five values using the worksheet below.

Then document the positive impact of achieving your goal of overcoming your eating behaviours on each of your top five values.

Refer to the values list below for ideas (you can also include your own if they are not listed here)

Accomplishment	Expertise	Making a difference
Accuracy	Expressiveness	Perfection
Adventure	Fairness	Positivity
Altruism	Faith	Power
Ambition	Family	Preparedness
Belonging	Fidelity	Professionalism
Calmness	Fitness	Recognition
Caring	Freedom	Reliability
Challenge	Friendship	Resourcefulness
Cheerfulness	Fun	Respect
Community	Generosity	Security
Compassion	Growth	Self-control
Competitiveness	Happiness	Selflessness
Consistency	Hard work	Sensitivity
Contentment	Harmony	Serenity
Contribution	Health	Spirituality
Control	Honesty	Stability

Cooperation	Humility	Strength
Courage	Independence	Structure
Creativity	Inner harmony	Success
Decisiveness	Insightfulness	Support
Dependability	Intellectual status	Teamwork
Discipline	Joy	Thankfulness
Discovery	Justice	Thoroughness
Efficiency	Kindness	Thoughtfulness
Empathy	Knowledge	Timeliness
Enjoyment	Leadership	Tolerance
Enthusiasm	Love	Trust
Equality	Loyalty	Vitality

Values – what's important to you? Examples	What is the positive impact of reaching my goal on this value?
freedom	Goal to overcome binge eating will help me to achieve freedom in my life
family	Goal to overcome binge eating will give me more headspace to be present with my family
1	
2	
3	
4	
5	

Life is Not a Dress Rehearsal

You have just one chance to live the life you want to live, but it's likely that your relationship with food and your body has been stopping you. Perhaps you have put off going on holiday, swimming, trying out a dance class, buying new clothes, going out with friends or to parties?

To create true happiness in your life, make it your mission to expose yourself to activities that really bring you joy. You may feel a great deal of anxiety about doing these things in the body you have now. However, stepping out of your comfort zone is like stretching a muscle – uncomfortable initially but necessary for flexibility and growth. Letting anxiety dictate your actions will shrink your world further. If you push through your discomfort now, future challenges will become more manageable, and you can begin to enrich your life.

It can be helpful to consider how you want to be remembered. Would you like to see 'she was always dieting' engraved on your gravestone? Imagine you are at a ripe old age and looking back at your life. What do you think would give you a deep sense of fulfilment?

⚡ Action Step

FULFILMENT GOALS TASK

A fulfilment goal is an objective aimed at achieving personal satisfaction, contentment, or sense of fulfilment in your life.

What aspects of your life have you been holding off until you achieve a certain body size?

Complete the table below by compiling a list of fulfilment goals. Set yourself achievable targets, with small manageable steps, and then think when you might be able to achieve these. Schedule these steps into your diary.

Fulfilment Goals (aspects of your life to reintroduce and pursuits to start doing)	Steps	Scheduled

Revisit your checklist regularly in order to revise and update it in alignment with the objective to live your most fulfilling life.

⚡ Action Step

THERAPEUTIC JOURNALING

We have previously explored the food journal as a tool to understand your eating habits and patterns. You can take this a step further by integrating therapeutic writing into your daily routine.

Journal writing is a safe way to become more conscious of your thoughts, emotions, and life experiences, in addition to being a way to process your feelings and build emotional resilience[229]. Research indicates that journaling not only reduces anxiety and alleviates stress, but also improves sleep quality[230].

Therapeutic writing is not about creating flawless journal entries. It allows you to forget grammar rules and write without inhibition. If you tend to be a perfectionist, you might find this challenging, but it's an opportunity to increase self-awareness and potentially break free from the pressure of everything needing to be perfect in your life.

Decide what time of day will suit you best, just before bed works well for many people. Start by setting a timer for just 5 minutes each day to make this new habit more manageable.

You can use pen and paper (any notebook or journal of your choice) or even a computer or other device, though this is not recommended if journaling at bedtime.

Download printable pages for journaling at https://marcellerosenutrition.co.uk/book-resources)

If this kind of writing feels too overwhelming, you might prefer to begin with something more structured, as follows:

- Make a note of one thing that you are stressed or fearful about today.
- Record one action you can take to prevent or prepare for it.
- Note one reason why it's unlikely to be as distressing as you think.
- Write down one reason why you know you will be able to cope with it.
- Identify one potential positive aspect of the situation.

38. YOUR SUPPORTIVE CIRCLE

The presence of your closest friends and family members can offer invaluable support if you let them know what you need. However, it's essential to recognise that certain relationships can present obstacles that prevent you from moving forward.

It is important to identify which relationships are supportive, pinpoint those that are creating challenges, and communicate with your family and partner about how they can help you.

Ways they can help:
- Engage in non-food-related activities with you (they can avoid arranging all social activities around food)
- Join you in exercise, e.g. going for a walk
- Ask you how they can help
- Accept there may be lapses (it's normal for them to happen) and keep positive

What's unhelpful:
- Threatening or lecturing, e.g. 'you shouldn't be eating that'
- Having perfectionist expectations
- Buying and leaving trigger foods accessible around the home
- Suggesting unhealthy takeaways/leaving out food snacks, and so on
- Sabotage – a partner or family member may be anxious about what your journey will mean for them

It's not uncommon for my clients to discover that their partners (often subconsciously) sabotage their attempts to create change. It may be that your partner is concerned about how your new dietary choices will impact their own meal routines or worries about how your relationship will evolve as you overcome your challenges. Their apprehension may come from a desire to protect you from potential disappointment or a fear that it may make you unhappy. Their own personal struggles with eating and food may also secretly fuel their reluctance to see you succeed.

Sabotaging comments to look out for:
- An extra helping won't harm you
- You're becoming quite boring
- You're no fun any more
- Everyone else is having some
- Come on, just split this with me

☆ Client Story

Natalie

Identifying Her Husband as a Saboteur

Natalie and I had been working together for a few weeks when she began to gain an insight into her most challenging situations and environments. Her trigger foods were chips and sweets. She hadn't been buying these foods, but her husband had a habit of bringing home fish and chip takeaways without asking her first, which she then found hard to say no to. She realised that after having the chips, she didn't even enjoy them.

We discussed how Natalie could address this with her husband. She decided to explain to him politely, but directly, how important this process was to her. She asserted that it was unhelpful to bring home these foods and asked that he refrain from doing so until she felt comfortable to have these foods at home without triggering a binge.

Upon further reflection, Natalie realised that her husband believed he was overweight and wanted to make health-related changes. Natalie observed that, perhaps subconsciously, he didn't want her to take control, as it would leave him with no one to collude with when wanting to bring home a takeaway.

☆ Client Story

Laura

Overcoming Shame and Partner Support

Biscuits were a significant trigger food for Laura when she started working with me. She had been buying biscuits for her husband who enjoyed a biscuit or two when at home. Laura confessed she often needed to secretly replace whole packets of biscuits she had eaten, to avoid her husband knowing she'd been 'at them'. I asked Laura if she had explained to her husband how challenging this was for her. She was at first horrified at the idea and said she felt a great deal of shame about it. She thought her husband wouldn't understand and would think badly of her.

During a coaching session, I asked Laura to come up with some ideas to troubleshoot this situation. She decided that she would explain to her husband that it would be helpful if, for now, he kept the biscuits in his office (as she knew she wouldn't go in there to get them). When I asked Laura how this went, she said, 'It was absolutely fine – he didn't mind at all and was very happy to help out.'

⚡ Action Step

YOUR SUPPORTIVE CIRCLE PLANNING

Refer to the guidelines below to devise a plan. Decide who in your life can provide support and what they can do to help.

- Decide if you are better doing this with or without your partner's help!
- Identify the people in your life who can help you.
- Explain to your partner how they can help (if they are one of the chosen ones!) and be specific.
- Avoid giving your helper mixed messages – *I'm desperate for chocolate* whilst also saying *I want to eat healthily from now on.*
- Ask your partner to do the shopping (or do an online order) – provide a specific list.
- Get your partner to join you in some physical activity.
- Reflect on why someone may be putting pressure on you/acting as a saboteur.
- Resist any pressure to go for unhelpful foods by planning what you will do or say in advance.
- Be firm and direct with your answer if a 'food pusher' is pressurising you to eat. Repeat '**No thank you**' until they stop asking – you **do not** need to give them a reason.

39. BUILDING HEALTHY BOUNDARIES

Binge and emotional eaters tend to have people-pleasing traits. You might recognise this in yourself if you worry about offending or disappointing others. Maybe you believe that your well-being isn't a good enough reason to place your needs above the approval of others?

While the desire to make other people happy is not a bad thing, people-pleasers tend to take it to the extreme. They frequently say yes to requests when they want to say no, and their lack of healthy boundaries makes them susceptible to situations that can lead to unwanted eating episodes.

Whilst being clear with your boundaries may feel like you are being selfish, in reality, it helps to maintain self-esteem, preserving your energy and ensuring you prioritise self-care[231] [232]. Boundaries are guidelines or limits that you establish for yourself regarding what forms of behaviour, communication, and interaction is acceptable to you. Metaphorically speaking, you are placing a fence around your property to keep you safe.

Perhaps the most challenging aspect of establishing new boundaries is sticking to them, especially when faced with resistance from individuals who may not anticipate them. You might feel uncomfortable with unexpected reactions. However, by communicating your boundaries respectfully, it's important to recognise that you bear no responsibility in how others respond.

While it may be tempting to allow fear or guilt to get in the way, do keep practising and, with time, the process will become less challenging and more instinctive.

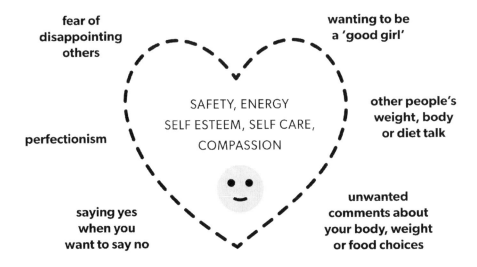

fear of disappointing others

wanting to be a 'good girl'

perfectionism

SAFETY, ENERGY
SELF ESTEEM, SELF CARE,
COMPASSION

other people's weight, body or diet talk

saying yes when you want to say no

unwanted comments about your body, weight or food choices

Other People's Body, Weight, or Diet Talk

Even if you now question the effectiveness of dieting, many people remain trapped within this mindset and see dieting as their only option. Regardless of where you are or who you're with, it's probable that someone will discuss their own body dissatisfaction, talk about their latest diet or weight loss, and maybe even comment on your weight.

For many women, it is their mothers who have been commenting on their body or weight throughout their life. It is likely they think this is normal, that it is being helpful, and comes from a place of love. If this has been the case for you, it's also quite plausible that your mother underwent a similar experience with her mother too. These patterns of behaviours and expectations are often subconsciously passed down through generations, making it difficult to change.

For many of the women I have worked with, their friends, family, and even work colleagues have made triggering comments that would easily throw them off course unless they put specific measures in place.

☆ **Client Story**

Sally

Need for Boundaries

Every time Sally visited her parents, her mum would say she was on a *'great new diet'* and wasn't it time that she tried it too as she hadn't lost any weight. *'Think how you will look after,'* she told her.

Sally was triggered by this conversation; she had been working hard on eating in a more balanced way and focusing on breaking her binge-restrict cycle. However, these remarks provided a cue for a cascade of automatic thoughts, *She's right you know, I should be losing weight, I've failed at every diet so far, this isn't working, what the hell is wrong with me?* And the thoughts went on…

The automatic thoughts triggered a stress response and a range of emotions including confusion, despair, and shame. When Sally arrived home, she would often decide to skip her next meal which led to bingeing by the end of the day.

Sally came to the realisation that she needed to establish clear boundaries with her mum and devise a proactive strategy for whenever her mother initiated this type of conversation.

If your family or friends have not done the work of dismantling diet culture in their life, they will continue to share their thoughts and beliefs with you and think that it is okay, so do expect it, but know that the next time they do, you will be prepared by working on the following exercise.

⚡ Action Step

BOUNDARY SETTING EXERCISE (FOR WEIGHT, DIET, AND BODY COMMENTS)

1. Firstly, give yourself compassion by reminding yourself that this might not be easy, but you are doing your best to manage these challenges.

2. Offer the 'offender' compassion. Remind yourself that they do not understand. They will need to go on their own journey to acknowledge the unintentional harm they may be causing.

3. Decide how you will respond to a specific person's comments in advance. Write down a prepared reframe and keep repeating it to yourself. (For Sally, this thought was something like; *My mum is still trapped in diet culture, but I don't have to be*).

4. Put your boundary in place:

Next time the person makes comments about your weight/body/food/diets, tell the person politely, firmly, and clearly that these discussions are a strictly no-go area. (If you are a people-pleaser – please remember that you have EVERY right to do so.)

You might want to say something like:

I find this conversation unhelpful and don't want to discuss my weight.

Or *How I look after my body is my choice.*

You can change the subject or even walk away from the conversation. Find a reason to remove yourself, such as going to the toilet or taking a stroll outside.

If someone gives you an inappropriate compliment, i.e. a remark intended to flatter that focuses on your physical appearance in a way that makes you feel uncomfortable or self-conscious, such as "You look so much better now that you've lost weight", a possible response could be:

Although I appreciate your good intentions, I would rather you didn't comment on my body.

If you struggle with this at first, you can try:

Thank you but... and shift the conversation on to something that feels more comfortable.

The 'offender' is unlikely to understand why you have responded differently to them, so it's important to reiterate your stance each time such a conversation arises. With persistence, this will eventually become clear to them.

Managing Weight Stigma in Healthcare

In addition to friends and family, medical professionals may also make unhelpful comments, as Donna's example illustrates below.

☆ Client Story

Donna

Managing Weight Stigma

Donna attended an appointment, with a doctor, about a skin condition that was unrelated to her weight.

Despite Donna's ongoing efforts and success in addressing her eating behaviour and adopting new health-promoting habits, the medical professional concentrated exclusively on her weight. Without offering any help for her skin condition, she referred Donna on to a weight loss programme.

Donna felt that she was neither listened to nor provided with equal treatment as someone who had the same health condition but happened to be in a smaller body. Given her history of food-related challenges, this experience was distressing and triggered unsettling emotions for her.

Donna knew that these remarks had the potential to throw her off course. She was therefore determined to have something prepared for next the time she faced a similar response from a medical professional.

The first thing to remember is that, as with any service provider, you expect fair and equal treatment. When you seek help from a medical professional, whether within the NHS or through private services, it is no different: you are essentially the customer. Some people may feel that they cannot voice their perspective during these sorts of interactions because the medical professional is the *expert* in the room. However, it's important to acknowledge that you are the expert of your own body, and it is only fair that you speak out if something doesn't feel quite right. You are entitled to ask questions during a consultation, challenge advice, and ask for a second opinion if you don't feel happy with the treatment offered.

You have the right to receive the same ethical, evidenced-based healthcare treatment as anyone else, to be treated with respect, and to state your own needs and opinions.

TIP: Have your responses prepared beforehand
Here are some suggestions[233]:

- *I do not wish to be weighed unless medically necessary (e.g. for correct dosage of medication)*
- *If you need my weight because it is medically necessary, please explain why, so I can give you my informed consent*
- *Please do not tell me my weight unless I request it*
- *I pursue healthy habits regardless of my weight status*
- *When you focus on my weight, it increases my stress levels and may lead me to relapse into disordered eating behaviours (if applicable), or lead to weight cycling, and that is not healthy for me*
- *Do people in smaller bodies suffer from this condition? If so, what advice and treatment would you offer them?*
- *Do you have any research evidence that you can share with me that the method of weight loss you are suggesting has worked for the majority of people in the long term (i.e. between 3-5 years)?*
- *In the limited time that we have for this appointment, I would like to focus on X*

Use your own discretion about which responses may be appropriate during your interaction.

40. NAVIGATING STRESS

Removing Stress or Managing It?

It's possible that binge or emotional eating has become your main coping mechanism for handling the everyday stresses of life.

While there are instances where we can proactively make changes to remove stress from our lives, such as changing jobs, seeking support for childcare, or ending an unhealthy relationship, this is not always feasible. We must acknowledge that external stressors will continue to be a part of life. The key is to acquire tools and strategies for effectively managing and navigating situations, instead of resorting to food as a way to cope. This chapter will provide you with various approaches to help you thrive on this journey, no matter what life throws at you.

Mindfulness, Breath Work, and Meditation

The idea of meditation does not sit well with everyone, so it is important to have an open mind and find the mindfulness, meditation, or breath work practice that you feel comfortable with. For beginners, I suggest starting with a simple breathing exercise, dedicating a few minutes each day. The key is finding a suitable time that works for you and consistently sticking to it.

If practised regularly, breath work can become an important tool to use when facing challenging situations[234]. It can help you manage your stress[235], sleep better, and improve your mood[236] [237] [238]. You are less likely to seek food to soothe if you make this part of your daily routine.

The aim is to understand how to transition from a *fight or flight* stress response to the *rest and digest* state of the parasympathetic nervous system.

⚡ Action Step

PRACTISE ALTERNATIVE STRATEGIES WITH THE STRESS TOOLKIT

I have provided various techniques and strategies below to help reduce stress and self-soothe. Find the tools that work best for you.

Breath Work[239][240]
Sit comfortably or lie down. You can shut your eyes if you wish, however, you can also do this with your eyes open. Your stomach should expand and fill with air when breathing in and then contract when breathing out.

In addition to your daily practice, use breath work when you notice specific symptoms of stress, such as tight shoulders, or an increase in your heart rate.

~**Cool air/Warm air** – Close your eyes, slowly breathe in through your nose and notice the air is cool. Slowly breathe out through your nose and notice the air feels warmer. Continue to do this whilst counting your breaths. What do you notice? Do you feel calmer?

~**Box breathing**: Breathe deep into your belly for 4 counts, pause for 4 counts, and then breath out for 4 counts. Repeat this 2-3 times.

~**A physiological sigh[241]**: Breathe twice through the nose – make the first inhale longer than the second, followed by an extended exhale through the mouth. (For example, inhale for 5 counts, and pause, then take a quick inhale for 1 second, pause for 3 seconds and exhale through your mouth for 6 seconds.) Repeat this 2-3 times.

Mindfulness & Meditation Techniques[242]

There are countless guided meditation and mindfulness apps available, and some are free to download. To incorporate a mindfulness practice into your daily routine, attach it to an existing habit at a time that suits you best. (For example, as soon as you wake in the morning, before getting out of bed.)

~5-4-3-2-1 grounding practice

This is a simple, yet powerful exercise designed to anchor yourself in the present moment by actively engaging all your senses.

Take a few deep breaths and ground yourself in the present moment. Pay attention to your breathing pattern and the movement of each breath in and out of your body. Notice how your abdomen and chest move in response to each breath.

Use these first moments to observe any unhelpful or racing thoughts in your mind. Tune into your current emotional state and notice the physical sensations in your body.

Then identify the following:

5 things you can see

4 things you can hear

3 things you can feel

2 things you can smell

1 thing you can taste

Take a moment to notice how you feel. Do you feel more calm and relaxed?

~Body scanning meditation

This mindfulness practice can help to reduce stress, promote relaxation, and deepen your mind-body connection.

1. Begin by finding a comfortable position, either sitting or lying down. Ensure that your body is relaxed and supported, with your spine comfortably straight if you're sitting. Close your eyes.

2. Take a few deep breaths to centre yourself, allowing each breath to be natural and effortless.

3. Begin the body scan by directing your attention to your feet. Notice any sensations you may feel in this area, such as warmth, tingling, or pressure. Spend a few moments observing these sensations without judgement.

4. Slowly move your attention upward, gradually scanning each part of your body. Pay attention to your ankles, calves, knees, thighs, hips, stomach, chest, back, shoulders, arms, hands, neck, and head. Take your time with each area, observing any sensations, tension, or relaxation you may encounter.

5. If you encounter areas of tension or discomfort, observe them with curiosity and try to relax that area on your exhale. Imagine the tension melting away with each breath, allowing the muscles to soften and release.

6. If your mind wanders, throughout the body scan, gently bring your focus back to the present moment and continue scanning.

7. When you've scanned your entire body, take a few moments to notice if you feel any different. Do you feel more calm or relaxed?

Daily Affirmations

Affirmations serve as positive, impactful statements that you say out loud to yourself every day. Starting your day with this practice, sets the tone for a more optimistic day. Keep your affirmations concise, positive, and phrased in the present tense, using "I am" instead of "I will".

Affirmation examples:

My feelings are valid, and I will give them my attention

I am worthy of investing in myself

I control my thoughts, my thoughts do not govern me

I can overcome any setback

I can do this

Gratitude Journaling

Studies have demonstrated that gratitude journaling can be used to help reduce anxiety and depression and may increase positive feelings and emotions[243][244].

How to begin:

Every day, write one thing you are grateful for in your journal – this can be as small or big as you want – such as *I'm grateful for the rain today to help my plants grow, I am grateful that I was able to make myself breakfast for the first time today*, or *I am grateful that I have a friend who asks how I am,* or similar. It can be especially powerful if you share this with a friend. You could partner up with someone and take turns to share something you are grateful for every day.

Time in Nature

Simply being out in nature (think parks, meadows, forests, and the like) and using your senses – seeing, hearing, smelling, touching – has several benefits[245] [246]. These include helping you to manage stress better, by lowering stress hormones, boosting the activity of your calming parasympathetic nervous system, and improving the quality of your sleep. Studies also suggest that time in nature reduces feelings of anxiety, depression, anger, and fatigue[247].

To enhance the benefits, you can try to mindfully focus in on your senses:

Notice what you see: Look at the shades of green and copper leaves, the vibrant colours and textures of wild plants and flowers, and the landscape around you.

Notice what you smell: Breathe in the scents and aromas of the grass, trees, plants, and flowers.

Notice what you hear: Listen for birds singing, the gentle rustling of leaves underfoot, trees swaying in the breeze, or the gentle patter of rain falling.

What can you feel? Run your hands along the textured bark of trees or feel the grass beneath your bare feet.

41. YOUR RELATIONSHIP WITH MOVEMENT

Not everyone finds pleasure in exercise, and it tends to be more appealing to those who excel at it. For many individuals, the idea of *any* physical activity is daunting, uncomfortable, and even distressing. You may face obstacles, such as finding sportswear that fits, mobility issues, joint pain, feelings of shame, or a negative association with exercise stemming from childhood (e.g. because you were shamed for not being good at sport at school).

It's worth noting that studies suggest that individuals who participate in physical activity tend to opt for healthier food options[248]. This may be linked to the release of endorphins, which can mitigate cravings for sugary foods, even in the presence of elevated hunger hormone levels.

Regularly moving your body can help improve self-esteem and body image and alleviate binge eating during stressful periods. It has many benefits for managing stress and improving sleep patterns[249]. Exercise is also thought to increase the brain's receptiveness to the satiety hormone leptin, meaning you will feel less hungry!

Activities such as walking, yoga, or Pilates will allow you to move your body more mindfully. These activities encourage you to be present in the moment, to focus on how you feel in your body, and can have a grounding effect. Walking in a green space will have added benefits, as discussed above, but it is also important to move for joy. This could be as simple as putting on your favourite song and dancing around your kitchen.

Flourishing or Punishing?

However, punishing, strenuous exercise will increase the release of stress hormones in your body and exercise can become unhealthy when it feels compulsive. If you think this may be an issue for you, it's important to be aware of some of the signs, such as restricting food *unless* you have exercised, working out as a justification to eat, or pushing yourself to exercise no matter what; for instance, if you are ill, exhausted, or have an injury. If this is the case, it's important to label thinking like this as a *diet mindset* thought and try to reframe it. (Refer back to chapter 31 as a reminder.)

It is therefore critical to get the balance right with physical activity:

- Avoid rewarding yourself with unhelpful food after exercising
- Activity does *not* have to mean working out at the gym
- Avoid using exercise to compensate for eating

How to Build Movement into Your Day

If you do not enjoy exercise, it's important to start with something simple and practical to fit in with your daily routine.

Begin with lifestyle activities such as parking your car at the far end of the car park, or away from the school gates. Opt for stairs instead of a lift at work, or get off the bus a stop earlier to do more walking. If you have a dog, ensure *you* are the family member to walk it a number of times in the week! Schedule regular walks, with family or friends, on a weekly basis.

Changes to the way we lead our lives – particularly influenced by technological advancements – have resulted in more sedentary lifestyle habits. Consider TV remote controls as an example. Rather than keeping the control nearby, place it at a distance so that standing up to change the channel adds in a small way to your daily activity!

Remember, as discussed in chapter 32, it can be helpful to add a movement habit to something you do all the time without thinking, e.g. do some press-ups against the wall each time you boil the kettle, or some squats every time you clean your teeth!

Moving After Your Meal

Movement after eating can reduce your blood glucose response by up to 50%, because when we move our muscles, it increases the amount of energy used and takes up more glucose from the blood[250]. Again, this doesn't mean doing intensive exercise, it can mean getting up to make a cuppa, doing the washing-up or having a short walk.

Ensure you take regular breaks from sitting every 30 minutes; this is in fact more beneficial than a one-hour gym workout followed by extended periods of sitting for the remainder of the day! If you are confined to a desk, stand up for periodic breaks, even if it's just to make a cup of tea.

⚡ Action Step

Relationship with Movement Task

If you're someone who says you don't enjoy exercise or movement, ask yourself the following and write it in the table provided below (A printable version can be downloaded at: https://marcellerosenutrition.co.uk/book-resources)

What is it I don't enjoy about exercise/movement?	
When did I stop enjoying it?	
What did I used to enjoy?	
What did I like about it then?	
Think of three achievable ways to get your body moving. *Please don't be unkind to yourself if it's something really simple.*	
Commit to ONE form of movement now and schedule it into your diary	
What will you tell yourself when you don't feel like doing it?	

Action Plan Summary

Focus on one action step at a time. Take your time to ensure you feel comfortable with each step before proceeding to the next one.

Action	What are you working on?	Duration	Chapter reference	Notes
Labelling your Feelings	Use the Feelings Chart to identify and name your feelings. This will help to strengthen your emotional intelligence and handle difficult feelings effectively. Record these emotions in your journal pages	Ongoing	34	
Self-Compassion Task	Use the journal pages to incorporate compassionate statements to improve self-compassion and build your self-worth	Ongoing	34	
Cravings List Tool	To help you meet your needs without using food to soothe	Ongoing	35	
Delay Response Strategy	Use this technique to delay acting on a craving	Ongoing	35	
Defusion Technique	To help manage cravings and challenging emotions and reduce binge or emotional eating events	Ongoing – this needs repetition to be effective	35	
Body Image Tasks	To help manage distress related to loathing your body which can prompt unwanted eating behaviours	Ongoing – as you work towards body acceptance	36	
Values Exercise	To help you shift your focus from dieting and weight loss thinking, instead building motivation and resilience, consistent behaviour patterns, and healthy boundaries	A one-off exercise. (Repeat annually for improved clarity over time)	37	

Action	What are you working on?	Duration	Chapter reference	Notes
Fulfilment Goals Task	To redirect your attention to your true purpose and begin living life in the present moment	Update regularly	37	
Therapeutic Journaling	A safe way to become more conscious of your thoughts, emotions, and life experiences in addition to being an outlet for processing your feelings and building emotional resilience	Ongoing	37	
Your Supportive Circle Planning	Decide who in your life can support you and what they can do to help	One-off exercise	38	
Boundary Setting Exercise (for weight, diet, and body comments)	Helps you manage potentially triggering situations and build self-worth. Set the boundaries and update when required	Ongoing – this requires practice!	39	
Practice Alternative Coping Strategies with the Stress Relief Toolkit	Find the options that work best for you to help reduce stress triggers and manage your eating behaviour	Ongoing	40	
Relationship with Movement Task	Find a way of moving your body that you enjoy and incorporate it into your weekly routine to manage stress, improve sleep, self-esteem/ body image and so on	Ongoing	41	

Step Into your Future

As you've read this book, you will have learnt that this journey won't always be a smooth, straightforward path. There will inevitably be obstacles and challenges when life presents situations that test you. That's why it's critical to have strategies in place to help you brush yourself off, get back on the bike, and continue on your path.

You will have laid the foundations to overcoming setbacks by:

- Eating regularly and in a way that supports your body and brain's nutritional needs
- Consistently repeating the strategies provided to manage your cravings
- Being aware of your triggers
- Working on other factors that may have been contributing to your eating behaviour
- Recognising changes in your thoughts, feelings, and behaviours
- Acquiring key strategies that can counter unhelpful patterns
- Having practical support from a friend or family member
- Improving your relationship with your body
- Creating healthy boundaries and building your self-worth

At certain points in the future, you may still be faced with *high-risk* situations that could potentially trigger a lapse. These might be anything, from trying on a pair of trousers which are too small, to an intensely emotional disagreement. Avoiding these situations might not always be possible or beneficial.

The key is to acknowledge that these situations will arise and to have a plan in place. Having a lapse docsn't mean you have failed. It should be seen as only a minor setback, perhaps occurring when you're unprepared for a high-risk situation.

Your journal can be a valuable tool here. By examining your *learning experiences*, you can understand how, when, and why the lapse occurred. What events or circumstances led up to it? How did you respond? Was it an 'I've blown it' response or were you able to move on?

Remember that catastrophic thinking is not helpful. It can decrease your motivation and belief in your ability to succeed. Essentially, it can determine whether a setback remains minor or escalates into something more significant. It's pivotal to develop the skill of learning how to manage your thoughts and emotions during and after a *learning experience*. Consistently reframing these thoughts with a more helpful statement can prevent you from falling back into the trap.

Creating your Master Plan – Your Core Self-Care Habits
Your core self-care habits will form part of your long-term strategy to keep you on track, no matter what comes your way in the future. Your journal will help you to identify and reflect on key aspects and high-risk situations in order to help you manage the ups and downs of life. Use the Master Plan template below as a working document to record your core self-care habits and update it when required. (A printable version is available to download at: https://marcellerosenutrition.co.uk/book-resources)

Your plan will be entirely individual to you, taking into account your own needs, situation, and lifestyle. However, I have provided a few examples of core self-care habits, below:

You have an evening class one night a week from 6-9 p.m. and become over hungry by the time you are home and graze on biscuits.

Core Self-Care Habit: Prep food in advance of my evening class in order to have a light meal before I go, and a balanced snack after the class.

You find it hard to manage your stress levels during the week and start the day feeling anxious and overwhelmed which often leads to stress eating.

Core Self-Care Habit: Do my breathing practice before I get out of bed, or do anything else, every morning. Set my alarm five minutes earlier to ensure this happens.

You often don't have time to make breakfast in the morning and this leads to a chaotic day of eating.

Core Self-Care Habit: Prep my overnight oats each evening while I'm making my dinner, so I have breakfast ready for the morning.

Master Plan	
Higher Risk Situations	**Core Self-Care Habit**

By prioritising these core self-care habits, you can establish a clear framework to guide you towards a life of freedom, reconnection, and joy. Now is the time to step into your future and embrace it.

A Final Thought

I hope that this book has helped guide you on your path to food and body freedom.

Allow your commitment to creating change empower you on your journey. Each step, no matter how small, is a significant step forward. Continue to challenge yourself each day, to pave your way towards the fulfilling life that you deserve.

Don't forget that you can join me in my Facebook group, The Food Freedom Collective, for your questions answered and for further support.

(facebook.com/groups/
thefoodfreedomcollectivewithmarcellerose)

You can also find further information and support here:

Instagram: @marcellerosenutrition

Website: marcellerosenutrition.co.uk

Facebook page: @marcellerosenutrition

Very Best Wishes,

Marcelle x

ADDITIONAL RESOURCES

Herb/spice	Foods to use it with	Other spices/herbs that combine well
Allspice	Beef, lamb, apples, beetroot, carrots, cabbage, squash, sweet potato, turnip Breads, desserts, soups	Cardamon, nutmeg, cinnamon, cloves, ginger, mace
Basil	Cheese (mozzarella), chicken, fish, pork, aubergine, courgette, pepper, potato, tomato Dry rubs, marinades, salad dressings, sauces, soups, stews, Italian dishes	Garlic, marjoram, oregano, rosemary, thyme
Bay leaves	Shellfish, beans, lentils, mushrooms, potatoes, tomatoes Bolognaise, risotto, soups, stews	Marjoram, oregano, sage, thyme
Cardamon	Chicken, duck, pork, lentils, carrots, citrus, corn, peas, sweet potato, squash, rice Curries	Cinnamon, cumin, ginger, turmeric
Cayenne pepper/ chilli powder	Chicken, beef, fish, aubergine, corn, courgette, potato, pepper, tomato, rice Marinades, salad dressings, sauces, soups, stews	Cumin, paprika, cinnamon
Cinnamon	Chicken, lamb, apple, carrot, pear, orange, sweet potato, squash Fruit, desserts, bread	Allspice, cloves, nutmeg

Cloves	Lamb, apples, beetroot, squash, sweet potato, tomato Breads, curries, soups, marinades, desserts	Cinnamon, nutmeg, allspice, basil
Coriander	Chicken, beef, fish, pork, tofu, onion, pepper, potato, tomato Dry rubs, curries, marinades, salads, sauces, soups, stews, stuffing	Chilli powder, cumin, cinnamon
Cumin	Beef, chicken, fish, pork, beans, lentils, tofu, rice Dry rubs, curries, marinades, soups, sauces	Cinnamon, garlic, ginger, oregano, turmeric
Garlic	Beef, chicken, fish, beans, tofu, cabbage, carrot, courgette, mushroom, tomato Dressings, dry rubs, curries, marinades, sauces, soups, stews, stir-fries	Cumin, coriander, ginger, rosemary, turmeric, oregano
Ginger	Beef, chicken, fish, pork, tofu, beetroot, carrot, citrus, sweet potato, squash Dressings, curries, marinades, stir-fries	Allspice, garlic, cardamon, cumin, turmeric
Mint	Middle Eastern dishes, lamb	
Nutmeg	Lamb, broccoli, cabbage, carrot, cauliflower, sweet potato, rice Stuffing, sauces	Allspice, cloves
Oregano	Chicken, fish, lamb, pork, beans, artichoke, courgette, mushroom, pepper, potato, tomato Dry rubs, marinades, salad dressings, sauces, soups	Bay leaves, basil, chilli powder, cumin, garlic, rosemary, thyme

Paprika	Chicken, lamb, shellfish, tofu, broccoli, cauliflower, squash, pepper, potato Marinades, rice, salad dressings, soups	Cardamon, chilli powder, cinnamon, cumin, garlic
Parsley	Fish Middle Eastern dishes	
Rosemary	Chicken, fish, lamb, pork, beans, mushroom, onion, peas, potato Dry rubs, marinades, sauces, soups, stews	Basil, garlic, oregano, thyme
Thyme	Beef, chicken, fish, lamb, pork, lentils, carrot, cauliflower, courgette, green beans, peas, tomatoes Dry rubs, marinades, salad dressings, soups, stews	Basil, bay leaves, oregano, rosemary
Turmeric	Chicken, fish, tofu, beans, lentils, cabbage, cauliflower, potato, sweet potato, rice Curries, soups, stews	Cardamon, cumin, garlic, ginger

Salad Dressings, Sauces, and Dips

Simple home-made sauces, dips, and dressings can transform the simplest of dishes in next to no time adding flavour and texture to your food. For dressings add all ingredients to a glass jar and shake, and keep in the fridge for another day (most will last up to a week).

Basic lemon dressing

3 tbsp olive oil
3 tbsp lemon juice
Salt & pepper

Basic balsamic dressing

2 tbsp olive oil
4 tbsp balsamic vinegar
(Optional ½ tsp mustard & ¼ tsp pure maple syrup)

Asian sesame dressing

2 tbsp sesame oil
2 tbsp tamari sauce
6 tbsp lemon juice

Works with any salad!

Harissa dressing

2 tbsp harissa paste
1 tbsp pure maple syrup
Juice of 1 lemon
3 tbsp extra virgin olive oil

Works well with a chickpea or bean salad

Cashew cream

100 g cashew nuts (soaked in boiling water for 5 min. to soften)
Zest and juice of 2 limes
½ garlic clove
4 tbsp water
Season

Works well in fish or chicken tacos

Avocado dressing

1 avocado
½ cup cashews
½ cup coriander
½–¾ cup water
Juice of 2 limes
1 tsp chilli powder
¼–½ tsp cayenne (optional)
Season

Works well in fish/chicken tacos

Tahini dressing

3½ tbsp tahini
1½ tbsp lemon juice
2 tbsp water – start with a little and add more if needed while stirring
(Optional 1 small clove garlic – crushed)

Delicious over roasted vegetable and quinoa salads

Tahini yoghurt sauce

200 g Greek style natural yoghurt
2 tbsp tahini
1 large garlic clove, crushed
Zest and juice of 1 lemon
Pinch of chilli flakes

Works well over roasted vegetable salad

Everyday vinaigrette

100 ml extra virgin olive oil
2 tbsp apple cider vinegar
1 tsp Dijon mustard
Pinch of salt

Great with any salad!

Dill and mustard

200 ml extra virgin olive oil
2 tbsp white wine vinegar
1 tsp grainy mustard
1 tsp Dijon mustard
1 tbsp honey
1 tsp chopped dill
1 tbsp spring onions, finely chopped
1 clove garlic, grated

Great in potato salad, with fish, or sautéed vegetables

Chilli and lemon zest

4 tbsp olive oil
2 tbsp white wine vinegar
1 lemon, zested
½ fresh red chilli, very finely diced (or ½ tsp chilli flakes)
1 small garlic clove, grated
Pinch of salt

Miso tahini

3 tbsp tahini
2 tbsp apple cider vinegar
25 ml warm water
1 tbsp tamari or soy sauce
1 tsp white miso (optional)

Hazelnut and parsley

4 tbsp extra virgin olive oil
2 tbsp red wine vinegar
25 g toasted hazelnuts, finely chopped
1 bunch fresh parsley, finely chopped
Pinch of salt

Ginger and coriander

1 tbsp toasted sesame oil
2 tbsp apple cider vinegar
2 tbsp coriander leaves, finely chopped
½ red chilli, deseeded & finely diced (or ½ tsp chilli flakes)
1 garlic clove, grated
1 tsp fresh ginger, peeled & finely grated
1 tbsp brown sugar of choice
Pinch of salt

Works well with a chickpea or bean salad

Raita

200g natural yoghurt (or plain coconut yoghurt for dairy-free option)
1 red onion, finely chopped
½ cucumber, finely chopped
½ pack coriander, finely chopped
1 lemon squeezed

Great with chicken tikka and other curry dishes

Cheat spicy mayo alternative

4 tbsp natural yoghurt (or plain coconut yoghurt for dairy-free option)
1 tsp sweet smoked paprika

Great as a dip or in tacos

Micronutrients, Their Impact and Where to Find Them in Food		
Micronutrient	**Impact on mood, stress, energy, and eating behaviour**	**Which foods**
Magnesium	Used by the 'batteries' inside each body cell (known as mitochondria) to produce energy from food. It supports our adrenal glands to help us cope with the stress that may trigger uncontrolled eating episodes and also helps to maintain balanced blood glucose, to keep mood stable, and to avoid crashes and sugar cravings[251][252].	Almonds, barley, black-eyed peas, Brazil nuts, brown rice, butter beans, cocoa, cod, eggs, figs, kidney beans, molasses, parsnips, spinach, soya beans, Swiss chard, quinoa, seeds
B Vitamins	Needed to manufacture brain chemicals. B1, B2, and B3 are required for the conversion of food to energy. B3 deficiency is associated with anxiety. Folate and B12 also help to improve energy levels, as they are essential for the production of red blood cells that carry oxygen around the body. When energy is low, we are far more likely to reach for a less helpful, quick energy fix snack. B5 supports our adrenals to help with stress management. NB You are at greater risk of low vitamin B status if you regularly drink alcohol.	B1(thiamine) – asparagus, legumes, meat, nuts, pork, rye, whole grains B2(riboflavin) – asparagus, avocados, broccoli, beans, eggs, dairy products, liver, nuts, sprouts, whole grains B3 (niacin) – chicken, eggs, fish, legumes, meat, nuts, seeds B5 (pantothenic acid) – avocado, eggs, green vegetables, organ meats, lentils, dairy, mushrooms, sweet potato, whole grains B6 (pyridoxine), folate (B9), B12 – dairy, eggs, fish, meat, poultry, seafood (See chapter 19 if vegetarian or vegan)

Iron	Crucial for the structure and function of the central nervous system. It is used by cell 'batteries' to turn food into energy and is also needed for haemoglobin to carry oxygen around the body. Low iron status can have a significant impact on energy, and motivation to take action be low with insufficient levels. NB Iron along with selenium, zinc, and iodine are also essential for thyroid health. An underactive thyroid can result in a myriad of symptoms including fatigue and low mood.	Asparagus, cauliflower, dark green leafy vegetables, leeks, green peas, nuts, seeds, beans, lentils, whole grains, meat, eggs
Chromium	Supports blood glucose regulation and helps to prevent cravings.	Beans, broccoli, asparagus, mushrooms, pepper, green beans, apple, tomatoes, prunes, banana, whole grains, beef, liver, eggs, meat, poultry, chicken, seafood
Zinc	Supports thyroid function (see iron), the production of brain chemicals, and hormonal balance[253] [254]	Dairy, egg, ginger, lentils, meat, tofu, seeds, seafood whole grains
Vitamin C	Plays a potential role in mood and anxiety. Known to be most abundant in the brain, where it is believed to be involved with neuroprotection, neurotransmission, and neuromodulation[255] [256].	Berries, broccoli, Brussel sprouts, cabbage, citrus fruit, parsley, papaya, peppers, sweet potatoes, tomatoes
Vitamin D	Involved in transmitting brain chemicals and low levels are linked to low mood.	Dairy, eggs, mushrooms, oily fish NB Sun exposure is one of the best ways to increase your levels, but this is only at certain times of the year depending on the climate where you live

Omega-3 Fatty Acids	Essential for the structure and function of the brain and counteracts the appetite enhancing effects of omega-6 fatty acids	Oily fish, chia seeds, flax seeds, walnuts NB Some people are unable to convert the plant-based forms of omega-3 into DHA and EPA that the brain needs. Oily fish provides DHA and EPA directly
Amino Acids[257] **(the building blocks of protein)**	**L-carnitine** Helps the conversion of fats to energy within the cells. Helps with improved efficiency of energy activity within muscles.	Beef, chicken, fish, milk, liver
	Cysteine Makes n-acetyl cysteine (NAC) which supports the thyroid and blood glucose levels.	Eggs, meat, fish, whole grains
	L-theanine A role in reducing stress and improving mood-increasing levels of serotonin, dopamine, and the calming brain chemical GABA.	Beef, beans, chicken, cottage cheese, eggs, fish, garlic, green tea, liver, seafood
	Tryptophan Required to make melatonin, which plays a role in sleep, and the brain chemical serotonin. Low serotonin levels can trigger cravings, low mood, and depression[258] [259].	Dairy, meat, bananas, beans, fish, lentils, oats, poultry, seeds
Other	**Choline** Forms acetylcholine, a calming brain chemical that may play a role in suppressing appetite and is responsible for many nervous system functions[260] [261].	Eggs, meat, fish, shitake mushrooms, whole grains

REFERENCES

1   Perelman, H., Gilbert, K., Grilo, C.M. and Lydecker, J.A. (2023). Loss of control in binge-eating disorder: Fear and resignation. *International Journal of Eating Disorders*.

2   Andrés, A. and Saldaña, C. (2014). Body dissatisfaction and dietary restraint influence binge eating behavior. *Nutrition Research*, 34(11), pp.944–950.

3   Brytek-Matera, A., Bronowicka, P. and Walilko, J. (2021). Restraint theory: Significance of rumination. *European Psychiatry*, [online] 64(S1), pp.S179–S180.

4   Andrés, A. and Saldaña, C. (2014). Body dissatisfaction and dietary restraint influence binge eating behavior. *Nutrition Research*, 34(11), pp.944–95.

5   Grilo, C. and Masheb, R. (2000). Onset of dieting vs binge eating in outpatients with binge eating disorder. *International Journal of Obesity*, 24(4), pp.404–409.

6   Fazzino, T.L., Rohde, K. and Sullivan, D.K. (2019). Hyper-Palatable Foods: Development of a Quantitative Definition and Application to the US Food System Database. *Obesity*, 27(11), pp.1761–1768.

7   Westwater, M.L., Fletcher, P.C. and Ziauddeen, H. (2016). Sugar addiction: the state of the science. *European Journal of Nutrition*, [online] 55(S2), pp.55–69.

8   Epstein, L.H., Temple, J.L., Roemmich, J.N. and Bouton, M.E. (2009). Habituation as a determinant of human food intake. *Psychological Review*, [online] 116(2), pp.384–407.

9   Schaefer, L.M., Hazzard, V.M. and Wonderlich, S.A. (2022). Treating eating disorders in the wake of trauma. *The Lancet Child & Adolescent Health*, 6(5), pp.286–288.

10   Brytek-Matera, A., Bronowicka, P. and Walilko, J. (2021). Restraint theory: Significance of rumination. *European Psychiatry*, [online] 64(S1), pp.S179–S180.

11   Stice, E., Agras, W. S., Telch, C. F., Halmi, K. A., Mitchell, J. E. and Wilson, T. (2001). Subtyping binge eating-disordered women along dieting and negative affect dimensions. *The International Journal of Eating Disorders*, 30(1), 11-27.

12   Andrés, A. and Saldaña, C. (2014b). Body dissatisfaction and dietary restraint influence binge eating behavior. *Nutrition Research*, 34(11), pp.944–950.

13   Stice E, Burger K. (2015). Dieting as a risk factor for eating disorders. *The Wiley handbook of eating disorders*, pp. 312–323.

14   Bhutani, S., Kahn, E., Tasali, E. and Schoeller, D.A. (2017). Composition of two-week change in body weight under unrestricted free-living conditions. *Physiological Reports*, [online] 5(13), p.e13336.

15   Corbin, K.D., Carnero, E.A., Dirks, B., Igudesman, D., Yi, F., Marcus, A.K., Davis, T., Pratley, R.E., Rittmann, B.E., Krajmalnik-Brown, R. and Smith, S.R. (2023). Host-diet-gut microbiome interactions influence human energy balance: a randomized clinical trial. *Nature Communications*, 14(1).

16   Dounchis, J. Z., Karam, A. M., Stein, R. I. and Wilfley, D. E. (2021). Subtyping patients with binge-eating disorder by dietary restraint and negative affect: Characteristics and treatment outcome. *Journal of Consulting and Clinical Psychology*, 89(12), 1020-1025.

17   Zheng, H., Lenard, N.R., Shin, A.C. and Berthoud, H.-R. (2009). Appetite control and energy balance regulation in the modern world: reward-driven brain overrides repletion signals. *International Journal of Obesity*, [online] 33(2), pp.S8–S13.

18   Fothergill, E. and Guo, J., et al. (2016). Persistent metabolic adaptation 6 years after 'The Biggest Loser' competition. *Obesity (Silver Spring, Md.)*, [online] 24(8), pp.1612–9.

19   Schueler, J., Philip, S., Vitus, D., Engler, S. and Fields, S.A. (2022). Group differences in binge eating, impulsivity, and intuitive and mindful eating among intermittent fasters and non-fasters. *Appetite*, p.106416.

20   Templeman, I., Smith, H.A., Chowdhury, E. and Chen, Y.-C, et al (2021a). A randomized controlled trial to isolate the effects of fasting and energy restriction on weight loss and metabolic health in lean adults. *Science Translational Medicine*, [online] 13(598).

21   Parra, D., Ramel, A., Bandarra, N., Kiely, M., Martinez, J.A. and Thorsdottir, I. (2008). A diet rich in long chain omega-3 fatty acids modulates satiety in overweight and obese volunteers during weight loss. *Appetite* 51, pp.676–80.

22   Darcey, V.L., Guo, J., Courville, A.B., Gallagher, I., Avery, J.A., W. Kyle Simmons, Ingeholm, J.E., Herscovitch, P., Martin, A. and Hall, K.D. (2023). Dietary fat restriction affects brain reward regions in a randomized crossover trial. *JCI insight*, [online] 8(12).

23   Albracht-Schulte, K., Kalupahana, N.S., Ramalingam, L., Wang, S., Rahman, S.M., Robert-McComb, J. and Moustaid-Moussa, N. (2018). Omega-3 fatty acids in obesity and metabolic syndrome: a mechanistic update. *The Journal of Nutritional Biochemistry*, 58, pp.1–16.

24   Rebello, C.J., O'Neil, C.E. and Greenway, F.L. (2016). Dietary fiber and satiety: the effects of oats on satiety. *Nutrition Reviews*, [online] 74(2), pp.131–147.

25   Giel, K.E., Zipfel, S., Alizadeh, M., Schäffeler, N., Zahn, C., Wessel, D., Hesse, F.W., Thiel, S. and Thiel, A. (2012). Stigmatization of obese individuals by human resource professionals: an experimental study. *BMC Public Health*, 12(1).

26   Flint, S.W., Čadek, M., Codreanu, S.C., Ivić, V., Zomer, C. and Gomoiu, A. (2016). Obesity Discrimination in the Recruitment Process: 'You're Not Hired!' *Frontiers in Psychology*, [online] 7(647).

27   Muennig, P. (2008). The body politic: the relationship between stigma and obesity-associated disease. *BMC Public Health*, 8(1).

28   Schvey, N.A., Puhl, R.M. and Brownell, K.D. (2011). The Impact of Weight Stigma on Caloric Consumption. *Obesity*, [online] 19(10), pp.1957–1962.

29   Durso, L.E., Latner, J.D., White, M.A., Masheb, R.M., Blomquist, K.K., Morgan, P.T. and Grilo, C.M. (2011). Internalized weight bias in obese patients with binge eating disorder: Associations with eating disturbances and psychological functioning. *International Journal of Eating Disorders*, [online] 45(3), pp.423–427.

30   Dohnt, H. and Tiggemann, M. (2006). The contribution of peer and media influences to the development of body satisfaction and self-esteem in young girls: A prospective study. *Developmental Psychology*, 42(5), pp.929–936.

31   Greenberg, B.S., Eastin, M., Hofschire, L., Lachlan, K. and Brownell, K.D. (2003). Portrayals of Overweight and Obese Individuals on Commercial Television. *American Journal of Public Health*, [online] 93(8), pp.1342-1348.

32   Ganipisetti, V.M. and Bollimunta, P. (2023). *Obesity and Set-Point Theory*. [online] PubMed. Available at: https://www.ncbi.nlm.nih.gov/books/NBK592402/.

33   Keesey, R.E. (1978). Set-Points and Body Weight Regulation. *Psychiatric Clinics of North America*, 1(3), pp.523–543.

34   Rhee, E.-J. (2017). Weight Cycling and Its Cardiometabolic Impact. *Journal of Obesity & Metabolic Syndrome*, 26(4), pp.237–242.

35   Dankel, S.N., Degerud, E.M., Borkowski, K., Fjære, E., Midtbø, L.K., Haugen, C., Solsvik, M.H., Lavigne, A.M., Liaset, B., Sagen, J.V., Kristiansen, K., Mellgren, G. and Madsen, L. (2014). Weight cycling promotes fat gain and altered clock gene expression in adipose tissue in C57BL/6J mice. *American Journal of Physiology-Endocrinology and Metabolism*, 306(2), pp.E210–E224.

36   Simonds, S.E., Pryor, J.T. and Cowley, M.A. (2018). Repeated weight cycling in obese mice causes increased appetite and glucose intolerance. *Physiology & Behavior*, [online] 194, pp.184–190.

37   Yeung, A.Y. and Tadi, P. (2020). *Physiology, Obesity Neurohormonal Appetite And Satiety Control*. [online] PubMed. Available at: https://www.ncbi.nlm.nih.gov/books/NBK555906/.

38   Sumithran, P., Prendergast, L.A., Delbridge, E., Purcell, K., Shulkes, A., Kriketos, A. and Proietto, J. (2011). Long-Term Persistence of Hormonal Adaptations to Weight Loss. *New England Journal of Medicine*, 365(17), pp.1597–1604.

39   Mann, T., Tomiyama, A.J., Westling, E., Lew, A.-M., Samuels, B. and Chatman, J. (2007). Medicare's search for effective obesity treatments: Diets are not the answer. *American Psychologist*, [online] 62(3), pp.220–233.

40   Miller, W.C. (1999). How effective are traditional dietary and exercise interventions for weight loss? *Medicine & Science in Sports & Exercise*, 31(8), pp.1129–1134.

41   Bhutani, S., Kahn, E., Tasali, E. and Schoeller, D.A. (2017b). Composition of two-week change in body weight under unrestricted free-living conditions. *Physiological Reports*, [online] 5(13), p.e13336.

42   Kreitzman, S.N., Coxon, A.Y. and Szaz, K.F. (1992). Glycogen storage: illusions of easy weight loss, excessive weight regain, and distortions in estimates of body composition. *The American Journal of Clinical Nutrition*, 56(1), pp.292S-293S.

43   Masheb, R.M. and Grilo, C.M. (2006). Eating patterns and breakfast consumption in obese patients with binge eating disorder. *Behaviour Research and Therapy*, 44(11), pp.1545–1553.

44   D'Adamo, L., Linardon, J., Manasse, S.M. and Juarascio, A.S. (2024). Trajectories of therapeutic skills use and their dynamic relations to symptom change during cognitive-behavioral therapy for bulimia nervosa. *The International Journal of Eating Disorders*, [online] 57(1), pp.173–183.

45   Basolo, A., Bechi Genzano, S., Piaggi, P., Krakoff, J. and Santini, F. (2021). Energy Balance and Control of Body Weight: Possible Effects of Meal Timing and Circadian Rhythm Dysregulation. *Nutrients*, 13(9), p.3276.

46   Flanagan, A., Bechtold, D.A., Pot, G.K. and Johnston, J.D. (2020). Chrono-nutrition: From molecular and neuronal mechanisms to human epidemiology and timed feeding patterns. *Journal of Neurochemistry*, 157(1), pp.53–72.

47   Luhovyy, B.L. and Kathirvel, P. (2022). *Chapter Five – Food proteins in the regulation of blood glucose control.* [online] ScienceDirect.

48   Simpson, S.J. and Raubenheimer, D. (2005). Obesity: the protein leverage hypothesis. *Obesity Reviews*, 6(2), pp.133–142.

49   Pham et al. Plasma Amino Acid Appearance and Status of Appetite Following a Single Meal of Red Meat or a Plant-Based Meat Analog: A Randomized Crossover Clinical Trial. Curr Dev Nutr. May 2022.

50   Neufingerl, N. and Eilander, A. (2021). Nutrient Intake and Status in Adults Consuming Plant-Based Diets Compared to Meat-Eaters: A Systematic Review. *Nutrients*, [online] 14(1), p.29.

51   Bakaloudi, D.R., Halloran, A., Rippin, H.L., Oikonomidou, A.C., Dardavesis, T.I., Williams, J., Wickramasinghe, K., Breda, J. and Chourdakis, M. (2020). Intake and adequacy of the vegan diet. A systematic review of the evidence. *Clinical Nutrition*, [online] 40(5).

52   Geiselman, P. J. and Novin, D. (1982). The Role of Carbohydrates on Appetite, Hunger and Obesity. *Appetite: Journal for Intake research*, 3, pp.203-23.

53   Hulshof, T., de Graaf, C. and Weststrate, J.A. (1993). The Effects of Preloads Varying in Physical State and Fat Content on Satiety and Energy Intake. *Appetite*, 21(3), pp.273–286.

54   Valk, R., Hammill, J. and Grip, J. (2022). Saturated fat: villain and bogeyman in the development of cardiovascular disease? *European Journal of Preventive Cardiology*, 29 (18), pp.2312–2321.

55   Halasz, G., Parati, G. and Piepoli, M.F. (2022b). Editorial comments: Focus on atherosclerosis. *European Journal of Preventive Cardiology*, 29(18), pp.2283–2285.

56   Martínez-González, M.A., Gea, A. and Ruiz-Canela, M. (2019). The Mediterranean Diet and Cardiovascular Health. *Circulation Research*, [online] 124(5), pp.779–798.

57   Dighriri, I.M., Alsubaie, A.M., Hakami, F.M., ST et al. (2022). Effects of Omega-3 Polyunsaturated Fatty Acids on Brain Functions: A Systematic Review. *Cureus*, [online] 14(10).

58   Wang, H., Storlien, L.H. and Huang, X.-F. (2002). Effects of dietary fat types on body fatness, leptin, and ARC leptin receptor, NPY, and AgRP mRNA expression. *American Journal of Physiology-Endocrinology and Metabolism*, 282(6), pp.E1352–E1359.

59   Haber, G.B., Heaton, K.W., Murphy, D. and Burroughs, L.F. (1977). Depletion and disruption of dietary fibre. *The Lancet*, 310(8040), pp.679–682.

60   Rebello, C.J., O'Neil, C.E. and Greenway, F.L. (2016). Dietary fiber and satiety: the effects of oats on satiety. *Nutrition Reviews*, [online] 74(2), pp.131–147.

61   Aguilera, J.M. (2018). The food matrix: implications in processing, nutrition and health. *Critical Reviews in Food Science and Nutrition*, 59(22), pp.3612–3629.

62   Forde, C.G. and de Graaf, K. (2022). Influence of Sensory Properties in Moderating Eating Behaviours and Food Intake. *Frontiers in Nutrition*, 9.

63   Zijlstra, N., de Wijk, R., Mars, M., Stafleu, A. and de Graaf, C. (2009). Effect of bite size and oral processing time of a semisolid food on satiation. *The American Journal of Clinical Nutrition*, 90(2), pp.269–275.

64   Rebello, C.J., O'Neil, C.E. and Greenway, F.L. (2016b). Dietary fiber and satiety: the effects of oats on satiety. *Nutrition Reviews*, [online] 74(2), pp.131–147. doi:https://doi.org/10.1093/nutrit/nuv063.

65   Perrier, E.T., Johnson, E.C., McKenzie, A.L., Ellis, L.A. and Armstrong, L.E. (2015). Urine colour change as an indicator of change in daily water intake: a quantitative analysis. *European Journal of Nutrition*, [online] 55(5), pp.1943–1949.

66   Lunn, J. and Foxen, R. (2008). How much water do we really need? *Nutrition Bulletin*, 33(4), pp.336–342.

67   Haber, G.B., Heaton, K.W., Murphy, D. and Burroughs, L.F. (1977). Depletion and disruption of dietary fibre. *The Lancet*, 310(8040), pp.679–682.

68   Klevebrant, L. and Frick, A. (2022). Effects of caffeine on anxiety and panic attacks in patients with panic disorder: a systematic review and meta-analysis. *General Hospital Psychiatry*, [online] 74(74), pp.22–31.

69   Lovallo, W.R., Whitsett, T.L., al'Absi, M., Sung, B.H., Vincent, A.S. and Wilson, M.F. (2005). Caffeine Stimulation of Cortisol Secretion across the Waking Hours in Relation to Caffeine Intake Levels. *Psychosomatic Medicine*, 67(5), pp.734–9.

70   Reichert, C.F., Deboer, T. and Landolt, H. (2022). Adenosine, caffeine, and sleep–wake regulation: state of the science and perspectives. *Journal of Sleep Research*, 31(4).

71   Colrain, I.M., Nicholas, C.L. and Baker, F.C. (2014). Alcohol and the sleeping brain. *Handbook of Clinical Neurology*, [online] (125), pp.415–431.

72   Ebrahim, I.O., Shapiro, C.M., Williams, A.J. and Fenwick, P.B. (2013). Alcohol and Sleep I: Effects on Normal Sleep. *Alcoholism: Clinical and Experimental Research*, 37(4), pp.539–549.

73   Azevedo, L.D.S., de Souza, A.P.L., Ferreira, I.M.S., Lima, D.W. da C. and Pessa, R.P. (2020). Binge eating and alcohol consumption: an integrative review. *Eating and Weight Disorders – Studies on Anorexia, Bulimia and Obesity*, 26(3), pp.759–769.

74   Herman, C.Peter. and Polivy, J. (1990). From dietary restraint to binge eating: Attaching causes to effects. *Appetite*, 14(2), pp.123–125.

75   Peters, A., Schweiger, U., Pellerin, L., Hubold, C., Oltmanns, K.M., Conrad, M., Schultes, B., Born, J. and Fehm, H.L. (2004). The selfish brain: competition for energy resources. *Neuroscience & Biobehavioral Reviews*, 28(2), pp.143–180.

76   Maki, K.C. and Phillips, A.K. (2015). Dietary Substitutions for Refined Carbohydrate That Show Promise for Reducing Risk of Type 2 Diabetes in Men and Women. *The Journal of Nutrition*, [online] 145(1), pp.159S163S.

77   Page, K.A., Seo, D., Belfort-DeAguiar, R., Lacadie, C., Dzuira, J., Naik, S., Amarnath, S., Constable, R.T., Sherwin, R.S. and Sinha, R. (2011). Circulating glucose levels modulate neural control of desire for high-calorie foods in humans. *Journal of Clinical Investigation*, 121(10), pp.4161–4169.

78   Fernstrom, J.D. and Wurtman, R.J. (1971). Brain Serotonin Content: Increase Following Ingestion of Carbohydrate Diet. *Science*, 174(4013), pp.1023–1025.

79   Wurtman, R.J. and Wurtman, J.J. (1986). Carbohydrate craving, obesity and brain serotonin. *Appetite*, 7, pp.99–103.

80   Galen, K.A., Horst, K.W. and Serlie, M.J. (2021). Serotonin, food intake, and obesity. *Obesity Reviews*, 22(7).

81   Gasmi, A., Nasreen, A., Menzel, A., Gasmi Benahmed, A., Pivina, L., Noor, S., Peana, M., Chirumbolo, S. and Bjørklund, G. (2023). Neurotransmitters Regulation and Food Intake: The Role of Dietary Sources in Neurotransmission. *Molecules*, [online] 28(1), p.210.

82   Vucetic, Z. and Reyes, T.M. (2010). Central dopaminergic circuitry controlling food intake and reward: implications for the regulation of obesity. *Wiley Interdisciplinary Reviews: Systems Biology and Medicine*, 2(5), pp.577–593.

83   Frank, G.K.W. (2013). Altered Brain Reward Circuits in Eating Disorders: Chicken or Egg? *Current Psychiatry Reports*, 15(10).

84   Gasmi, A., Nasreen, A., Menzel, A., Gasmi Benahmed, A., Pivina, L., Noor, S., Peana, M., Chirumbolo, S. and Bjørklund, G. (2023). Neurotransmitters Regulation and Food Intake: The Role of Dietary Sources in Neurotransmission. *Molecules*, [online] 28(1), p.210.

85   Mathur, K., Agrawal, R.K., Nagpure, S. and Deshpande, D. (2020). Effect of artificial sweeteners on insulin resistance among type-2 diabetes mellitus patients. *Journal of Family Medicine and Primary Care*, [online] 9(1), pp.69–71.

86   Suez, J. and Y., Valdés-Mas, et al. (2022). Personalized microbiome-driven effects of non-nutritive sweeteners on human glucose tolerance. *Cell*, [online] 185(18), pp.S0092-8674(22)009199.

87   Pepino, M.Y., Tiemann, C.D., Patterson, B.W., Wice, B.M. and Klein, S. (2013). Sucralose affects glycemic and hormonal responses to an oral glucose load. *Diabetes care*, [online] 36(9), pp.2530–5.

88   Suez, J. and Korem, T., et al. (2014). Artificial sweeteners induce glucose intolerance by altering the gut microbiota. *Nature*, [online] 514(7521), pp.181–6.

89   Yunker, A.G. and Alves, J.M., et al. (2021). Obesity and Sex-Related Associations With Differential Effects of Sucralose vs Sucrose on Appetite and Reward Processing: A Randomized Crossover Trial. *JAMA Network Open*, [online] 4(9), pp.e2126313–e2126313.

90   Hulshof, T., de Graaf, C. and Weststrate, J.A. (1993b). The Effects of Preloads Varying in Physical State and Fat Content on Satiety and Energy Intake. *Appetite*, 21(3), pp.273–286.

91   Bhardwaj, R.L., Parashar, A., Parewa, H.P. and Vyas, L. (2024). An Alarming Decline in the Nutritional Quality of Foods: The Biggest Challenge for Future Generations' Health. *Foods*, [online] 13(6), p.877. doi:https://doi.org/10.3390/foods13060877.

92   Liu, S., Cheng, L., Liu, Y., Zhan, S., Wu, Z. and Zhang, X. (2023). Relationship between Dietary Polyphenols and Gut Microbiota: New Clues to Improve Cognitive Disorders, Mood Disorders and Circadian Rhythms. *Foods*, [online] 12(6), p.1309.

93   MacLean, P.S., Blundell, J.E., Mennella, J.A. and Batterham, R.L. (2017). Biological control of appetite: A daunting complexity. *Obesity*, 25, pp.S8–S16.

94   Faulconbridge, L.F. and Hayes, M.R. (2011). Regulation of Energy Balance and Body Weight by the Brain: A Distributed System Prone to Disruption. *The Psychiatric clinics of North America*, [online] 34(4), pp.733–745.

95   Cooper, C.B., Neufeld, E.V., Dolezal, B.A. and Martin, J.L. (2018). Sleep deprivation and obesity in adults: A brief narrative review. BMJ *Open Sport & Exercise Medicine*, [online] 4(1), pp.e000392.

96   De Leon, A., A and Hanlon, E., C (2020). Impact of Sleep Restriction on Food Intake and Food Choice. *Neurological Modulation of Sleep*, pp.217–228.

97   Pan, W. and Kastin, A.J. (2014). Leptin: A biomarker for sleep disorders? *Sleep Medicine Reviews*, 18(3), pp.283–290.

98   Thau, L., Gandhi, J. and Sharma, S. (2023). *Physiology, cortisol.* [online] National Library of Medicine. Available at: https://www.ncbi.nlm.nih.gov/books/NBK538239/.

99   McEwen, B.S., Nasca, C. and Gray, J.D. (2015). Stress Effects on Neuronal Structure: Hippocampus, Amygdala and Prefrontal Cortex. *Neuropsychopharmacology*, [online] 41(1), pp.3–23.

100 Peters, A., Kubera, B., Hubold, C. and Langemann, D. (2011). The Selfish Brain: Stress and Eating Behavior. *Frontiers in Neuroscience*, 5.

101 Austin, J. and Marks, D. (2009). Hormonal Regulators of Appetite. *International Journal of Pediatric Endocrinology*, [online] 2009, pp.1–9.

102 Austin, J. and Marks, D. (2009). Hormonal Regulators of Appetite. *International Journal of Pediatric Endocrinology*, [online] 2009, pp.1–9.

103 www.wegovy.com. (n.d.). *Wegovy® Side Effects | Wegovy® (semaglutide) Injection 2.4 mg.* [online] Available at: https://www.wegovy.com/taking-wegovy/side-effects.html.

104 Wilding, J.P.H. and Batterham, R.L., *et al* (2022). Weight regain and cardiometabolic effects after withdrawal of semaglutide: The STEP 1 trial extension. *Diabetes, Obesity and Metabolism*, [online] 24(8), pp.1553–1564.

105 Austin, J. and Marks, D. (2009b). Hormonal Regulators of Appetite. *International Journal of Pediatric Endocrinology*, [online] 2009, pp.1–9.

106 Austin, J. and Marks, D. (2009b). Hormonal Regulators of Appetite. *International Journal of Pediatric Endocrinology*, [online] 2009, pp.1–9.

107   Schumacher, M. and Mattern, C., et al. (2014). Revisiting the roles of progesterone and allopregnanolone in the nervous system: Resurgence of the progesterone receptors. *Progress in Neurobiology*, 113, pp.6–39.

108   Khalil, J., Boutros, S., Kheir, N., Kassem, M., Salameh, P., Sacre, H., Akel, M., Obeid, S. and Hallit, S. (2022). Eating disorders and their relationship with menopausal phases among a sample of middle-aged Lebanese women. *BMC Women's Health*, 22(1).

109   Baker, J.H. and Runfola, C.D. (2016). Eating disorders in midlife women: A perimenopausal eating disorder? *Maturitas*, 85, pp.112–116.

110   Krishnan, S., Tryon, R., Welch, L.C., Horn, W.F. and Keim, N.L. (2016). Menstrual cycle hormones, food intake, and cravings. *The FASEB Journal*, 30(S1).

111   Littman, E., Dean, J.M., Wagenberg, B. and Wasserstein, J. (2021). ADHD in Females Across the Lifespan and the Role of Estrogen. *The ADHD Report*, 29(5), pp.1–8.

112   Ptacek, R. and Stefano, G., et al. (2016). Attention deficit hyperactivity disorder and disordered eating behaviors: links, risks, and challenges faced. *Neuropsychiatric Disease and Treatment*, 12, p.571.

113   Research Blog. (2018). *Understanding the Link Between ADHD and Binge Eating Could Point to New Treatments.* [online] Available at: https://researchblog.duke.edu/2018/03/13/binge-eating-disorder/.

114   Seymour, K.E., Reinblatt, S.P., Benson, L. and Carnell, S. (2015). Overlapping neurobehavioral circuits in ADHD, obesity, and binge eating: evidence from neuroimaging research. *CNS Spectrums*, 20(4), pp.401–411.

115   National Institute of Mental Health (2023). *Attention-Deficit/Hyperactivity Disorder.* [online] www.nimh.nih.gov. Available at: https://www.nimh.nih.gov/health/topics/attention-deficit-hyperactivity-disorder-adhd.

116   Fusar-Poli, P., Rubia, K., Rossi, G., Sartori, G. and Balottin, U. (2012). Striatal dopamine transporter alterations in ADHD: pathophysiology or adaptation to psychostimulants? A meta-analysis. *The American Journal of Psychiatry*, [online] 169(3), pp.264–72.

117   Cani, P.D., Van Hul, M., Lefort, C., Depommier, C., Rastelli, M. and Everard, A. (2019). Microbial regulation of organismal energy homeostasis. *Nature Metabolism*, [online] 1(1), pp.34–46.

118   Foster, J.A. and McVey Neufeld, K.-A. (2013). Gut–brain axis: how the microbiome influences anxiety and depression. *Trends in Neurosciences*, 36(5), pp.305–312.

119   Alcock, J., Maley, C.C. and Aktipis, C.A. (2014). Is eating behavior manipulated by the gastrointestinal microbiota? Evolutionary pressures and potential mechanisms. *BioEssays*, 36(10), pp.940–949.

120   Peat, C.M., Huang, L., Thornton, L.M., Von Holle, A.F., Trace, S.E., Lichtenstein, P., Pedersen, N.L., Overby, D.W. and Bulik, C.M. (2013). Binge eating, body mass index, and gastrointestinal symptoms. *Journal of Psychosomatic Research*, [online] 75(5), pp.456–461.

121   Peters, J.E., Basnayake, C., Hebbard, G.S., Salzberg, M.R. and Kamm, M.A. (2021). Prevalence of disordered eating in adults with gastrointestinal disorders: A systematic review. *Neurogastroenterology & Motility*.

122   Peat, C.M., Huang, L., Thornton, L.M., Von Holle, A.F., Trace, S.E., Lichtenstein, P., Pedersen, N.L., Overby, D.W. and Bulik, C.M. (2013b). Binge eating, body mass index, and gastrointestinal symptoms. *Journal of Psychosomatic Research*, [online] 75(5), pp.456–461.

123   Trefflich, I., Marschall, H.-U. and Giuseppe, R. di, et al. (2019). Associations between Dietary Patterns and Bile Acids—Results from a Cross-Sectional Study in Vegans and Omnivores. *Nutrients*, 12(1), p.47.

124   Ioniță-Mîndrican, C.-B., Ziani, K., Mititelu, M., Oprea, E., Neacșu, S.M., Moroșan, E., Dumitrescu, D.-E., Roșca, A.C., Drăgănescu, D. and Negrei, C. (2022). Therapeutic Benefits and Dietary Restrictions of Fiber Intake: A State of the Art Review. *Nutrients*, [online] 14(13), p.2641.

125   Liu, S., Cheng, L., Liu, Y., Zhan, S., Wu, Z. and Zhang, X. (2023). Relationship between Dietary Polyphenols and Gut Microbiota: New Clues to Improve Cognitive Disorders, Mood Disorders and Circadian Rhythms. *Foods*, [online] 12(6), p.1309.

126   van de Wouw, M., Schellekens, H., Dinan, T.G. and Cryan, J.F. (2017). Microbiota-Gut-Brain Axis: Modulator of Host Metabolism and Appetite. *The Journal of Nutrition*, 147(5), pp.727–745. doi:https://doi.org/10.3945/jn.116.240481.

127   Howland, R.H. (2014). Vagus Nerve Stimulation. *Current Behavioral Neuroscience Reports*, [online] 1(2), pp.64–73.

128   Gierthmuehlen, M. and Plachta, D.T.T. (2015). Effect of selective vagal nerve stimulation on blood pressure, heart rate and respiratory rate in rats under metoprolol medication. *Hypertension Research*, 39(2), pp.79–87.

129   Pramanik, T., Sharma, H.O., Mishra, S., Mishra, A., Prajapati, R. and Singh, S. (2009). Immediate effect of slow pace bhastrika pranayama on blood pressure and heart rate. *Journal of Alternative and Complementary Medicine (New York, N.Y.)*, [online] 15(3), pp.293–295.

130   Browning, K.N. and Travagli, R.A. (2014). Central Nervous System Control of Gastrointestinal Motility and Secretion and Modulation of Gastrointestinal Functions. *Comprehensive Physiology*, [online] 4(4), pp.1339–1368.

131   Aaronson, S.T. and Sears, P., et al. (2017). A 5-Year Observational Study of Patients With Treatment-Resistant Depression Treated With Vagus Nerve Stimulation or Treatment as Usual: Comparison of Response, Remission, and Suicidality. *American Journal of Psychiatry*, 174(7), pp.640–648.

132   Aaronson, S.T. and Sears, P., et al. (2017). A 5-Year Observational Study of Patients With Treatment-Resistant Depression Treated With Vagus Nerve Stimulation or Treatment as Usual: Comparison of Response, Remission, and Suicidality. *American Journal of Psychiatry*, 174(7), pp.640–648.

133   Rosenberg, S. (2017). *Accessing the healing power of the vagus nerve : self-help exercises for anxiety, depression, trauma, and autism.* Berkeley, California: North Atlantic Books.

134   Mäkinen, T.M. and Mäntysaari, et al. (2008). Autonomic Nervous Function During Whole-Body Cold Exposure Before and After Cold Acclimation. *Aviation, Space, and Environmental Medicine*, 79(9), pp.875–882.

135   Kinoshita, T., Nagata, S., Baba, R., Kohmoto, T. and Iwagaki, S. (2006). Cold-water face immersion per se elicits cardiac parasympathetic activity. *Circulation Journal: Official Journal of the Japanese Circulation Society*, [online] 70(6), pp.773–776.

136   Jungmann, M., Vencatachellum, S., Van Ryckeghem, D. and Vögele, C. (2018). Effects of Cold Stimulation on Cardiac-Vagal Activation in Healthy Participants: Randomized Controlled Trial. *JMIR Formative Research*, [online] 2(2).

137   Vickhoff, B., Malmgren, H., Åström, R., Nyberg, G., Ekström, S.-R., Engwall, M., Snygg, J., Nilsson, M. and Jörnsten, R. (2013). Music structure determines heart rate variability of singers. *Frontiers in Psychology*, [online] 4.

138   Gao, J., Leung, H.K., Wu, B.W.Y., Skouras, S. and Sik, H.H. (2019). The neurophysiological correlates of religious chanting. *Scientific Reports*, [online] 9(1), pp.1–9.

139   Mason, H. and Vandoni, M., et al. (2013). Cardiovascular and Respiratory Effect of Yogic Slow Breathing in the Yoga Beginner: What Is the Best Approach? *Evidence-Based Complementary and Alternative Medicine*, [online] 2013, pp.1–7.

140   Van Cauter, E., Polonsky, K.S. and Scheen, A.J. (1997b). Roles of Circadian Rhythmicity and Sleep in Human Glucose Regulation*. *Endocrine Reviews*, 18(5), pp.716–738.

141   Stenvers, D.J., Scheer, F.A.J.L., Schrauwen, P., la Fleur, S.E. and Kalsbeek, A. (2018). Circadian clocks and insulin resistance. *Nature Reviews Endocrinology*, [online] 15(2), pp.75–89.

142   Yoshimura, M., Flynn, B.P., Kershaw, Y.M., Zhao, Z., Yoichi Ueta, Lightman, S.L. and Conway-Campbell, B. (2023). Phase-shifting the circadian glucocorticoid profile induces disordered feeding behaviour by dysregulating hypothalamic neuropeptide gene expression. *Communications biology*, 6(1).

143   Zeman, M., Okuliarova, M. and Valentina Sophia Rumanova (2023). Disturbances of Hormonal Circadian Rhythms by Light Pollution. *International Journal of Molecular Science*, 24(8), pp.7255–7255.

144   Antunes, L.C., Levandovski, R., Dantas, G., Caumo, W. and Hidalgo, M.P. (2010). Obesity and shift work: chronobiological aspects. *Nutrition Research Reviews*, [online] 23(1), pp.155–168.

145   Ishihara, A., Courville, A.B. and Chen, K.Y. (2023). The Complex Effects of Light on Metabolism in Humans. *Nutrients*, 15(6), pp.1391–1391.

146   Potter, G.D.M., Cade, J.E., Grant, P.J. and Hardie, L.J. (2016a). Nutrition and the circadian system. *British Journal of Nutrition*, [online] 116(3), pp.434–442.

147   De Young, K.P. and Bottera, A.R. (2022). A biobehavioral circadian model of restrictive eating and binge eating. *International Journal of Eating Disorders*.

148   Vujović, N. and Piron, M.J., et al. (2022b). Late isocaloric eating increases hunger, decreases energy expenditure, and modifies metabolic pathways in adults with overweight and obesity. *Cell Metabolism*, [online] 34(10), pp.1486–1498.e7.

149   Basolo, A., Bechi Genzano, S., Piaggi, P., Krakoff, J. and Santini, F. (2021). Energy Balance and Control of Body Weight: Possible Effects of Meal Timing and Circadian Rhythm Dysregulation. *Nutrients*, 13(9), p.3276.

150   Flanagan, A., Bechtold, D.A., Pot, G.K. and Johnston, J.D. (2020). Chrono-nutrition: From molecular and neuronal mechanisms to human epidemiology and timed feeding patterns. *Journal of Neurochemistry*, 157(1), pp.53–72.

151   Potter, G.D.M., Skene, D.J., Arendt, J., Cade, J.E., Grant, P.J. and Hardie, L.J. (2016). Circadian Rhythm and Sleep Disruption: Causes, Metabolic Consequences, and Countermeasures. *Endocrine Reviews*, 37(6), pp.584–608.

152   Calderón-Asenjo R.E., and Jalk-Muñoz, M.C. et al (2022). Association Between Emotional Eating, Sociodemographic Characteristics, Physical Activity, Sleep Duration, and Mental and Physical Health in Young Adults. *Journal of Multidisciplinary Healthcare*, Volume 15, pp.2845–2859.

153   Frank, S., Gonzalez, K., Lee-Ang, L., Young, M.C., Tamez, M. and Mattei, J. (2017). Diet and Sleep Physiology: Public Health and Clinical Implications. *Frontiers in Neurology*, 8(393).

154   Goldstein, A.N. and Walker, M.P. (2014). The Role of Sleep in Emotional Brain Function. *Annual Review of Clinical Psychology*, [online] 10(1), pp.679–708.

155   Knutson, K.L., Spiegel, K., Penev, P. and Van Cauter, E. (2007). The metabolic consequences of sleep deprivation. *Sleep Medicine Reviews*, [online] 11(3), pp.163–178.

156   Knutson, K.L., Spiegel, K., Penev, P. and Van Cauter, E. (2007). The metabolic consequences of sleep deprivation. *Sleep Medicine Reviews*, [online] 11(3), pp.163–178.

157   Anderson, C. and Platten, C.R. (2011). Sleep deprivation lowers inhibition and enhances impulsivity to negative stimuli. *Behavioural Brain Research*, 217(2), pp.463–466.

158   Reichert, C.F., Deboer, T. and Landolt, H. (2022). Adenosine, caffeine, and sleep–wake regulation: state of the science and perspectives. *Journal of Sleep Research*, 31(4).

159   Cao, Y., Zhen, S., Taylor, A., Appleton, S., Atlantis, E. and Shi, Z. (2018). Magnesium Intake and Sleep Disorder Symptoms: Findings from the Jiangsu Nutrition Study of Chinese Adults at Five-Year Follow-Up. *Nutrients*, [online] 10(10), p.1354.

160   Arab, A., Rafie, N., Amani, R. and Shirani, F. (2022). The role of magnesium in sleep health: A systematic review of available literature. *Biological Trace Element Research*, [online] 201(1).

161   Abboud, M. (2022). Vitamin D Supplementation and Sleep: A Systematic Review and Meta-Analysis of Intervention Studies. *Nutrients*, 14(5), p.1076.

162   Petrus, P. and Cervantes, M., et al. (2022). Tryptophan metabolism is a physiological integrator regulating circadian rhythms. *Molecular Metabolism*, [online] 64, p.101556.

163   Richard, D.M., Dawes, M.A., Mathias, C.W., Acheson, A., Hill-Kapturczak, N. and Dougherty, D.M. (2009). L-Tryptophan: Basic Metabolic Functions, Behavioral Research and Therapeutic Indications. *International journal of tryptophan research : IJTR*, [online] 2, pp.45–60.

164   Vujović, N. and Piron, M.J., et al. (2022). Late isocaloric eating increases hunger, decreases energy expenditure, and modifies metabolic pathways in adults with overweight and obesity. *Cell Metabolism*, [online] 34(10), pp.1486-1498.e7.

165   Vujović, N. and Piron, M.J., et al. (2022). Late isocaloric eating increases hunger, decreases energy expenditure, and modifies metabolic pathways in adults with overweight and obesity. *Cell Metabolism*, [online] 34(10), pp.1486-1498.e7.

166   Al-Karawi, D. and Jubair, L. (2016). Bright light therapy for nonseasonal depression: Meta-analysis of clinical trials. *Journal of Affective Disorders*, 198, pp.64–71.

167   Evelyna Kambanis, P., Bottera, A.R. and De, K.P. (2023). Responses to bright light exposure in individuals with binge-spectrum eating disorders characterized by high dietary restraint and negative affect. *International Journal of Eating Disorders*, 56(12), pp.2250–2259.

168   Beauchamp, M.T. and Lundgren, J.D. (2016). A Systematic Review of Bright Light Therapy for Eating Disorders. *The Primary Care Companion For CNS Disorders*.

169   Hashimoto, S., Kohsaka, M., Nakamura, K., Honma, H., Honma, S. and Honma, K. (1997). Midday exposure to bright light changes the circadian organization of plasma melatonin rhythm in humans. *Neuroscience Letters*, 221(2-3), pp.89–92.

170   Reichert, C.F., Deboer, T. and Landolt, H. (2022). Adenosine, caffeine, and sleep–wake regulation: state of the science and perspectives. *Journal of Sleep Research*, 31(4).

171   Colrain, I.M., Nicholas, C.L. and Baker, F.C. (2014). Alcohol and the sleeping brain. *Handbook of Clinical Neurology*, [online] (125), pp.415–431.

172   Wolniczak, I. and Cáceres-Del Aguila, J.A.,et al. (2013). Association between Facebook Dependence and Poor Sleep Quality: A Study in a Sample of Undergraduate Students in Peru. PLoS ONE, [online] 8(3), p.e59087.

173   Andrés, A. and Saldaña, C. (2014). Body dissatisfaction and dietary restraint influence binge eating behavior. *Nutrition Research*, 34(11), pp.944–950.

174   Tricò, D., Filice, E., Trifirò, S. and Natali, A. (2016). Manipulating the sequence of food ingestion improves glycemic control in Type 2 diabetic patients under free-living conditions. *Nutrition & Diabetes*, 6(8), pp.e226–e226.

175   Dunn, C., Haubenreiser, M., Johnson, M., Nordby, K., Aggarwal, S., Myer, S. and Thomas, C. (2018). Mindfulness Approaches and Weight Loss, Weight Maintenance, and Weight Regain. *Current Obesity Reports*, 7(1), pp.37–49.

176   Wein, H. (2015). *Restricting Sugary Food May Lead to Overeating.* [online] National Institutes of Health (NIH). Available at: https://www.nih.gov/news-events/nih-research-matters/restricting-sugary-food-may-lead-overeating.

177   Andrés, A. and Saldaña, C. (2014b). Body dissatisfaction and dietary restraint influence binge eating behavior. *Nutrition Research*, 34(11), pp.944–950.

178   Higgs, S. and Spetter, M.S. (2018) Cognitive Control of Eating: the role of memory in appetite and weight gain. *Current Obesity Reports* 7, PP.50-59

179   Dunn, C., Haubenreiser, M., Johnson, M., Nordby, K., Aggarwal, S., Myer, S. and Thomas, C. (2018). Mindfulness Approaches and Weight Loss, Weight Maintenance, and Weight Regain. *Current Obesity Reports*, 7(1), pp.37–49

180   Kuo, B. and Bhasin, M., Jacquart, J., et al. (2015). Genomic and Clinical Effects Associated with a Relaxation Response Mind-Body Intervention in Patients with Irritable Bowel Syndrome and Inflammatory Bowel Disease. PLOS ONE, 10(4), p.e0123861.

181   Cherpak, C.E. (2019). Mindful eating: a review of how the stress-digestion-mindfulness triad may modulate and improve gastrointestinal and digestive function. *Integrative Medicine: A Clinician's Journal*, 18(4), pp.48–53.

182   McLean, J.A., Barr, S.I., Prior, J.C. (2001) Cognitive dietary restraint is associated with higher urinary cortisol excretion in healthy premenopausal women. *Am J Clin Nutr*, 73, pp.7-12.

183   Dounchis, J. Z., Karam, A. M., Stein, R. I. and Wilfley, D. E. (2021). Subtyping patients with binge-eating disorder by dietary restraint and negative affect: Characteristics and treatment outcome. *Journal of Consulting and Clinical Psychology*, 89(12), 1020-1025.

184   Wilson, G.T., Wilfley, D.E., Agras, W.S. and Bryson, S.W. (2010). Psychological Treatments of Binge Eating Disorder. *Archives of General Psychiatry*, [online] 67(1), p.94.

185   Grilo, C.M., Ivezaj, V. and Gueorguieva, R. (2024). Overvaluation of shape/weight at posttreatment predicts relapse at 12-month follow-up after successful behaviorally-based treatment of binge-eating disorder. *The International Journal of Eating Disorders*, [online] 57(5), pp.1268–1273.

186   Wilson, G.T. (2011). Treatment of Binge Eating Disorder. *Psychiatric Clinics of North America*, 34(4), pp.773–783.

187   Brytek-Matera, A., Bronowicka, P. and Walilko, J. (2021). Restraint theory: Significance of rumination. *European Psychiatry*, [online] 64(S1), pp.S179–S180.

188   Aziz, J. (2017). Social media and body issues in young adults: an empirical study on the influence of Instagram use on body image and fatphobia in Catalan university students. *repositori.upf.edu*. [online] Available at: https://repositori.upf.edu/handle/10230/33255.

189   Keirns, N.G., Stout, M.E., Smith, C.E., Layman, H.M., Cole, K.L., Ciciolla, L. and Hawkins, M.A.W. (2022). Mindful Acceptance, not Awareness, Associated with Lower Food Susceptibility. *Eating and weight disorders* : EWD, [online] 27(4), pp.1481–1489.

190   Colle, L., Hilviu, D., Boggio, M., Toso, A., Longo, P., Abbate-Daga, G., Garbarini, F. and Fossataro, C. (2023). Abnormal sense of agency in eating disorders. *Scientific Reports*, [online] 13(1), p.14176.

191   Wein, H. (2015). *Restricting Sugary Food May Lead to Overeating.* [online] National Institutes of Health (NIH). Available at: https://www.nih.gov/news-events/nih-research-matters/restricting-sugary-food-may-lead-overeating.

192   Polivy, J. and Herman, C.P. (2020b). Overeating in Restrained and Unrestrained Eaters. *Frontiers in Nutrition*, 7.

193   Zoccola, P.M. and Dickerson, S.S. (2012). Assessing the relationship between rumination and cortisol: A review. *Journal of Psychosomatic Research*, 73(1), pp.1–9.

194   Wildes, J.E., Forbes, E.E. and Marcus, M.D. (2014). Advancing research on cognitive flexibility in eating disorders: The importance of distinguishing attentional set-shifting and reversal learning. *International Journal of Eating Disorders*, 47(3), pp.227–230.

195   Cash, T.F. and Pruzinsky, T. (2002). Familial influences on body image development. *Body Image: a handbook of theory, research, and clinical practice*. New York: Guilford Press.

196   Cash, T.F. and Pruzinsky, T. (2002). Familial influences on body image development. *Body Image: a handbook of theory, research, and clinical practice*. New York: Guilford Press.

197   Cash, T.F. (1995). Developmental teasing about physical appearance: Retrospective descriptions and relationships with body image. *Social Behavior and Personality: An International Journal*, 23(2), 123–129.

198   Ziemer, K.S., Lamphere, B.R., Raque-Bogdan, T.L. and Schmidt, C.K. (2018). A Randomized Controlled Study of Writing Interventions on College Women's Positive Body Image. *Mindfulness*, 10(1), pp.66–77.

199   Linardon, J., Moffitt, R., Anderson, C. and Tylka, T.L. (2024). Testing for longitudinal bidirectional associations between self-compassion, self-criticism, and positive body image components. *Body Image*, [online] 49, p.101722.

200   Krauss, S., Dapp, L.C. and Orth, U. (2023). The Link Between Low Self-Esteem and Eating Disorders: A Meta-Analysis of Longitudinal Studies. *Clinical Psychological Science*, 11(6), pp. 1141–1158.

201   Neff, K. (2010). Review of The mindful path to self-compassion: Freeing yourself from destructive thoughts and emotions. *British Journal of Psychology*, 101, 179-181.

202   Bandini, L., Sighinolfi, C., Menchetti, M., Morri, M., Ronchi, D. D. and Atti, A. R. (2013, July 8). 1111 – Assertiveness and eating disorders: the efficacy of a CBT group training. Preliminary findings. European Psychiatry.   https://www.sciencedirect.com/science/article/abs/pii/S0924933813762151.

203   Neff, K. D. (2011). Self-compassion, self-esteem, and well-being. *Social and Personality Compass*, 5, 1-12.

204   Neff, K.D. (2023). Self-Compassion: Theory, Method, Research, and Intervention. *Annual Review of Psychology*, [online] 74(1), pp.193–218.

205   Braun, T.D., Park, C.L. and Gorin, A. (2016). Self-compassion, body image, and disordered eating: A review of the literature. *Body Image*, 17, pp.117–131.

206   Serpell, L., Amey, R. and Kamboj, S. (2019). The role of self-compassion and self-criticism in binge eating behaviour. *Appetite*, 144, p.104470.

207   Carbonneau, N., Holding, A., Lavigne, G. and Robitaille, J. (2021).

Feel Good, Eat Better: The Role of Self-Compassion and Body Esteem in Mothers' Healthy Eating Behaviours. *Nutrients*, 13(11), p.3907.

208 Polivy, J. and Herman, C.P. (2020). Overeating in Restrained and Unrestrained Eaters. *Frontiers in Nutrition*, 7.

209 Brunswig, K.A., Penix, T.M. and O'Donohue, W. (2002). *Relapse Prevention*. [online] ScienceDirect. Available at: https://www.sciencedirect.com/science/article/abs/pii/B012343010000180X.

210 www.sciencedirect.com. (n.d.). *Abstinence Violation – an overview | ScienceDirect Topics*. [online] Available at: https://www.sciencedirect.com/topics/psychology/abstinence-violation.

211 Robinson, K. and Wade, T.D. (2021). Perfectionism interventions targeting disordered eating: A systematic review and meta-analysis. *International Journal of Eating Disorders*, 54(4),pp.473-487.

212 Stojek, M. and Shank, L.M., et al (2018). A systematic review of attentional biases in disorders involving binge eating. *Appetite*, [online] 123, pp.367–389.

213 Lane, A.S. and Roberts, C. (2022). Contextualised reflective competence: a new learning model promoting reflective practice for clinical training. BMC *Medical Education*, [online] 22(1).

214 Lally, P., van Jaarsveld, C.H.M., Potts, H.W.W. and Wardle, J. (2010). How are habits formed: Modelling habit formation in the real world. *European Journal of Social Psychology*, [online] 40(6), pp.998–1009.

215 Duhigg, C. (2014). *Power of Habit : Why We Do What We Do in Life and Business*. New York: Random House Trade Paperbacks.

216 Spudeit, W.A., Sulzbach, N.S., Bittencourt, M. de A., Duarte, A.M.C., Liang, H., Lino-de-Oliveira, C. and Marino-Neto, J. (2013). The behavioral satiety sequence in pigeons (Columba livia). Description and development of a method for quantitative analysis. *Physiology & Behavior*, 122, pp.62–71.

217 Guerrini-Usubini, A., Cattivelli, R., Scarpa, A., Musetti, A., Varallo, G., Franceschini, C. and Castelnuovo, G. (2023). The interplay between emotion dysregulation, psychological distress, emotional eating, and weight status: A path model. *International Journal of Clinical and Health Psychology*, 23(1), p.100338.

218 Taylor, J., B (2008). *My Stroke of Insight*. Penguin Putnam Inc.

219 Price, C.J. and Hooven, C. (2018b). Interoceptive Awareness Skills for Emotion Regulation: Theory and Approach of Mindful Awareness in Body-Oriented Therapy (MABT). *Frontiers in Psychology*, [online] 9(798).

220 McAtamney, K., Mantzios, M., Egan, H. and Wallis, D.J. (2023). A systematic review of the relationship between alexithymia and emotional eating in adults. *Appetite*, 180, p.106279.

221 Price, C.J. and Hooven, C. (2018). Interoceptive Awareness Skills for Emotion Regulation: Theory and Approach of Mindful Awareness in Body-Oriented Therapy (MABT). *Frontiers in Psychology*, [online] 9(798).

222 Linardon, J., Messer, M. and Tylka, T.L. (2023b). Functionality appreciation and its correlates: Systematic review and meta-analysis. *Body Image*, 45, pp.65–72.

223 Matheson, E.M., King, D.E. and Everett, C.J. (2012). Healthy lifestyle habits and mortality in overweight and obese individuals. *Journal of the American Board of Family Medicine : JABFM*, [online] 25(1), pp.9–15.

224 Hughes, V. (2013). The big fat truth. *Nature*, 497(7450), pp.428–430.

225 Hughes, V. (2013). The big fat truth. *Nature*, 497(7450), pp.428–430.

226 Nuttall, F.Q. (2015). Body Mass Index. *Nutrition Today*, [online] 50(3), pp.117–128.

227 Nuttall, F.Q. (2015). Body Mass Index. *Nutrition Today*, [online] 50(3), pp.117–128.

228 Tomiyama, A.J., Hunger, J.M., Nguyen-Cuu, J. and Wells, C. (2016). Misclassification of cardiometabolic health when using body mass index categories in NHANES 2005–2012. *International Journal of Obesity*, 40(5), pp.883–886.

229 Ziemer, K.S., Lamphere, B.R., Raque-Bogdan, T.L. and Schmidt, C.K. (2018). A Randomized Controlled Study of Writing Interventions on College Women's Positive Body Image. *Mindfulness*, 10(1), pp.66–77.

230 Pennebaker, J.W. (2017). Expressive Writing in Psychological Science. *Perspectives on Psychological Science*, 13(2), pp.226–229.

231 Anne Katherine (2000). *Boundaries : where you end and I begin.* Editorial: New York: Simon & Schuster.

232 Therapist Aid. (n.d.). *Therapy worksheets, tools, and handouts.* [online] Available at: http://therapistaid.com.

233 Chastain, R. (2013). *What to Say at the Doctor's Office.* [online] Dances With Fat. Available at: https://danceswithfat.org/2013/04/01/what-to-say-at-the-doctors-office/

234 Wanden-Berghe, R.G., Sanz-Valero, J. and Wanden-Berghe, C.

(2010). The Application of Mindfulness to Eating Disorders Treatment: A Systematic Review. *Eating Disorders*, 19(1), pp.34–48.

235   Ashhad, S., Kam, K., Negro, C.A.D. and Feldman, J.L. (2022b). Breathing Rhythm and Pattern and Their Influence on Emotion. *Annual Review of Neuroscience*, 45(1).

236   Ashhad, S., Kam, K., Negro, C.A.D. and Feldman, J.L. (2022). Breathing Rhythm and Pattern and Their Influence on Emotion. *Annual Review of Neuroscience*, 45(1).

237   Venditti, S., Verdone, L., Reale, A., Vetriani, V., Caserta, M. and Zampieri, M. (2020). Molecules of Silence: Effects of Meditation on Gene Expression and Epigenetics. *Frontiers in Psychology*, 11.

238   Hoge, E.A., Bui, E., Mete, M., Dutton, M.A., Baker, A.W. and Simon, N.M. (2022). Mindfulness-Based Stress Reduction vs Escitalopram for the Treatment of Adults With Anxiety Disorders: A Randomized Clinical Trial. *JAMA Psychiatry*, [online] 80(1), pp.13–21.

239   Steffen, P.R., Austin, T., DeBarros, A. and Brown, T. (2017). The Impact of Resonance Frequency Breathing on Measures of Heart Rate Variability, Blood Pressure, and Mood. *Frontiers in Public Health*, 5.

240   Ma, X., Yue, Z.-Q., Gong, Z.-Q., Zhang, H., Duan, N.-Y., Shi, Y.-T., Wei, G.-X. and Li, Y.-F. (2017). The Effect of Diaphragmatic Breathing on Attention, Negative Affect and Stress in Healthy Adults. *Frontiers in Psychology*, [online] 8(874), pp.1–12.

241   Balban, M.Y., Neri, E., Kogon, M.M., Weed, L., Nouriani, B., Jo, B., Holl, G., Zeitzer, J.M., Spiegel, D. and Huberman, A.D. (2023). Brief structured respiration practices enhance mood and reduce physiological arousal. *Cell Reports Medicine*, [online] 4(1).

242   Sun, Y., Ju, P., Xue, T., Ali, U., Cui, D. and Chen, J. (2023). Alteration of faecal microbiota balance related to long-term deep meditation. *General Psychiatry*, [online] 36(1), p.e100893.

243   Emmons, R.A. and McCullough, M. (2003). Counting blessings versus burdens: an experimental investigation of gratitude and subjective well-being in daily life. *Journal of personality and social psychology*.

244   Diniz, G., Korkes, L., Luca Schiliró Tristão, Rosangela Pelegrini, Patrícia Lacerda Bellodi and Wanderley Marques Bernardo (2023). The effects of gratitude interventions: a systematic review and meta-analysis. *Einstein (São Paulo)*, 21.

245   Li, Q. (2022). Effects of forest environment (Shinrin-yoku/Forest bathing) on health promotion and disease prevention —the Establishment

of 'Forest Medicine'–. *Environmental Health and Preventive Medicine*, 27(0), pp.43–43.

246 White, M.P., Alcock, I., Grellier, J., Wheeler, B.W., Hartig, T., Warber, S.L., Bone, A., Depledge, M.H. and Fleming, L.E. (2019). Spending at least 120 minutes a week in nature is associated with good health and wellbeing. *Scientific Reports*, [online] 9(1).

247 News, N. (2023). *Frequent Visits to Green Space Linked to Lower Use of Certain Prescription Meds*. [online] Neuroscience News. Available at: https://neurosciencenews.com/green-space-medications-22280/.

248 Calderón-Asenjo, R.E., Jalk-Muñoz, M.C., Calizaya-Milla, Y.E., Calizaya-Milla, S.E., Ramos-Vera, C. and Saintila, J. (2022). Association Between Emotional Eating, Sociodemographic Characteristics, Physical Activity, Sleep Duration, and Mental and Physical Health in Young Adults. *Journal of Multidisciplinary Healthcare*, Volume 15, pp.2845–2859.

249 Master, H., Annis, J., Huang, S., Beckman, J.A., Ratsimbazafy, F., Marginean, K., Carroll, R., Natarajan, K., Harrell, F.E., Roden, D.M., Harris, P. and Brittain, E.L. (2022). Association of step counts over time with the risk of chronic disease in the All of Us Research Program. *Nature Medicine*, [online] 28(11), pp.2301–2308.

250 Chacko, E. (2016). Exercising Tactically for Taming Postmeal Glucose Surges. *Scientifica*, 2016, pp.1–10.

251 Arab, A., Rafie, N., Amani, R. and Shirani, F. (2022). The role of magnesium in sleep health: A systematic review of available literature. *Biological Trace Element Research*, [online] 201(1).

252 Sartori, S.B., Whittle, N., Hetzenauer, A. and Singewald, N. (2012). Magnesium deficiency induces anxiety and HPA axis dysregulation: Modulation by therapeutic drug treatment. *Neuropharmacology*, [online] 62(1), pp.304–312.

253 Fukunaka, A., Fujitani, Y. (2018). Role of Zinc Homeostasis in the Pathogenesis of Diabetes and Obesity. *International Journal of Molecular Sciences*, 19(2), p.476.

254 Roohani, N., Hurrell, R., Kelishadi, R. and Schulin, R. (2013). Zinc and its importance for human health: An integrative review. *Journal of Research in Medical Sciences: The Official Journal of Isfahan University of Medical Sciences*, [online] 18(2), pp.144–157.

255 Moritz, B. (2020). The role of vitamin C in stress-related disorders. *The Journal of Nutritional Biochemistry*, [online] 85, p.108459.

256 Plevin, D. and Galletly, C. (2020). The neuropsychiatric effects of vitamin C deficiency: a systematic review. *BMC Psychiatry*, 20(1).

257 Gasmi, A., Nasreen, A., Menzel, A., Gasmi Benahmed, A., Pivina, L., Noor, S., Peana, M., Chirumbolo, S. and Bjørklund, G. (2023). Neurotransmitters Regulation and Food Intake: The Role of Dietary Sources in Neurotransmission. *Molecules*, [online] 28(1), p.210.

258 Richard, D.M., Dawes, M.A., Mathias, C.W., Acheson, A., Hill-Kapturczak, N. and Dougherty, D.M. (2009). L-Tryptophan: Basic Metabolic Functions, Behavioral Research and Therapeutic Indications. *International journal of tryptophan research* : IJTR, [online] 2, pp.45–60.

259 Petrus, P., Cervantes, M., Samad, M., Sato, T., Chao, A., Sato, S., Koronowski, K.B., Park, G., Alam, Y., Mejhert, N., Seldin, M.M., Monroy Kuhn, J.M., Dyar, K.A., Lutter, D., Baldi, P., Kaiser, P., Jang, C. and Sassone-Corsi, P. (2022). Tryptophan metabolism is a physiological integrator regulating circadian rhythms. *Molecular Metabolism*, [online] 64, p.101556.

260 Derbyshire, E. (2019). Could we be overlooking a potential choline crisis in the United Kingdom? *BMJ Nutrition, Prevention & Health*, [online] 2(2), pp.86–89.

261 Bourre, J.M. (2006). Effects of nutrients (in food) on the structure and function of the nervous system: update on dietary requirements for brain. Part 1: micronutrients. *The Journal of Nutrition, Health & Aging*, [online] 10(5), pp.377–385.

ACKNOWLEDGMENTS

I am deeply grateful to Professor Ros Herman for meticulously reviewing my manuscript. Your comments and questions have been invaluable in helping me communicate my ideas and method clearly to the reader.

A heartfelt thank you to Harriet Frew, Jinty Sheerin, Lou Hockings-Thompson, Kate Hudson-Hall, and Nicky Williams for taking the time to read the manuscript and for your encouraging words.

Thank you to Deanne Jade and Professor Julia Buckroyd for inspiring me and introducing me to the world of eating psychology. Your expertise and passion in this field have profoundly influenced my professional journey and shaped my approach to helping my clients.

A big thanks to Leslie Mello for designing the wonderful illustrations.

Finally, thank you to my family for your unwavering support and to my clients who inspire me to continue my work every day.

Disclaimer

The information in this book is designed to help readers make informed decisions about their health. It is not a substitute for medical treatment by a healthcare provider. If you have a medical condition or need medical advice, please consult your doctor.

The case histories presented in this book are anonymised and fictionalised compilations of representative cases, for illustrative purposes only. Any resemblance to persons, living or deceased, is purely coincidental.

INDEX

W

Y

Z

Printed in Great Britain
by Amazon

58806276R00160